The Life and Teaching of Jesus

The Life and Teaching of Jesus

James and Audrey Bentley

Longman Group UK Limited
Longman House
Burnt Mill, Harlow, Essex CM20 2JE, England
and Associated Companies throughout the world

First published 1986
Second impression 1987

ISBN 0 582 34312 7

Set in 11/12½ pt Rockwell Light, Linotron 202
Produced by Longman Group (FE) Limited
Printed in Hong Kong

Audrey W Bentley began her teaching career in a boys' public school. She subsequently taught in junior schools and in a 'special' school for difficult children. Today she is deputy head of the Brigidine Convent School in Windsor, having been senior mistress at the Church of England High School, Eccles.

Her qualifications include a certificate of education from the University of Leeds, and a B.Ed. from Manchester University. She was awarded an M.Ed. for a thesis on nineteenth-century religious education in a Lancashire mill town.

James Bentley has taught religion in junior and secondary schools, to mature students at Liverpool University, and at Eton College (where he was senior chaplain). He has also been Maurice Reckitt research fellow in Christian social thought at the University of Sussex.

He holds Oxford degrees in Modern History and Theology, an Oxford B.D., and a D.Phil. of the University of Sussex. His books include a life of Pastor Martin Niemöller.

Acknowledgements

We are grateful to the following for permission to reproduce copyright material:

The Literary Trustees of Walter de la Mare and The Society of Authors as their representative for an extract from the poem 'Here lies a most beautiful lady' by Walter de la Mare; the Oxford and Cambridge University Presses for extracts from *New English Bible* (c) 1970.
The Scripture quotations in this publication are from the Revised Standard Version of the Bible, copyrighted 1971 and 1952 by the Division of Christian Education of the National Council of the Churches of Christ in the USA.

The authors are grateful to the five regional Examining Boards for their help.

We are grateful to the following for permission to reproduce photographs: Bayerischen Staatsgemäldesammlungen, Alte Pinakothek, Munich, page 162; British Library, page 26; Mary Evans Picture Library, pages 7, 18 and 169; Mansell Collection, pages 4, 36, 72, 90, 129, 155, 158 and 165; National Galleries of Scotland, Edinburgh, page 29; Peter Newark's Western Americana and Historical Picture Library, page 79; Popperfoto, page 66; John Ryland's Library, University of Manchester, page 33; Ronald Sheridan's Photo Library, pages 45, 60, 62, 68 and 75; Stanley Spencer Gallery, Cookham-on-Thames, page 98.

Cover: St Catherine's Monastery, Mount Sinai.

Contents

Introduction

A famous preacher said of Jesus, 'Two thousand years ago there was One on earth who lived the grandest life that has ever been lived yet — a life that every thinking man, with deeper or shallower meaning, has agreed to call divine.'

This preacher (whose name was F W Robertson) exaggerated. Not everyone agrees or has agreed that Jesus was divine — least of all those who put him to death at the age of thirty-three. Yet in spite of his early death, the life and teaching of Jesus has had more influence than that of any other man or woman.

Jesus has influenced pacifists and revolutionaries alike. Camille Desmoulins, a French revolutionary, about to be condemned to death, said, 'I am thirty-three years old — the age of that good revolutionary Jesus — an age fatal to revolutionaries.' He was guillotined two days later. By contrast to those who have been inspired to revolution by Jesus, in our own century the Indian leader Mahatma Gandhi totally renounced violence under the influence of Jesus's Sermon on the Mount.

Clearly the life and teaching of Jesus is a complex as well as a very rewarding study. The more you study it, the more it comes alive. We have written this book because we believe that even if you are studying this subject for an examination, it can remain fascinating.

Few subjects are so important as this one. Thomas Jefferson, third president of the United States of America, declared that 'Of all the systems of morality, ancient and modern, which have come under my observation, none appears to me so pure as that of Jesus.' To us Jesus's morality is also controversial as well as inspiring. People argue — and even quarrel — about it. As this book shows, they did in his lifetime, as they do now. So we hope you will find the subject exciting.

To use this book properly you will need a Bible. Examining boards recommend the New English Bible. In our quotations we have not confined ourselves to this version, but we always use it in the questions at the end of chapters.

Audrey W Bentley
James Bentley

1 The Life and Teaching of Jesus a brief survey

Seven important features

A reasonably competent outline of the life and teaching of Jesus might include seven items:

1 The birth of Jesus, when shepherds adore him and wise men from the east bring him gifts.
2 Stories Jesus told, such as the tale of the prodigal son.
3 Jesus's teaching on the good life, as in his Sermon on the Mount, when he said that those who make peace will be called the children of God.
4 Jesus's belief in prayer, and especially the prayer which he taught his followers, beginning, 'Our Father . . .' now known as the Lord's Prayer.
5 Some miracles — for example, the time when a wedding party ran out of wine and Jesus made more out of water.
6 Jesus's trial and his cruel death.
7 The stories of how Jesus appeared to his followers after he had died.

This outline is accurate. It will have been learned from hymns, sung maybe at school; from the Christmas story of Jesus's birth; from what worshipping Christians have learned in church. But where do all these facts come from in the first place?

Basically what we know about Jesus comes from the four Gospels — by Matthew, Mark, Luke and John — found at the beginning of the New Testament. As we shall see, other information about Jesus is also available, but these four Gospels are the basis of nearly everything we know about him.

The four Gospels and the differences between them

At first sight each Gospel seems to be a straightforward outline of Jesus's life. But the moment we look more closely, this turns out not to be the case.

Take the seven items of Jesus's life we have just listed. The startling fact is that they do not occur in every Gospel:

Only Matthew

Only Luke

1 The story of the wise men bringing Jesus gifts is found only in Matthew's Gospel, and the story of the shepherds is only in Luke. Neither Mark nor John tells us anything about Jesus's childhood.

Parables in Luke

2 Jesus obviously told many stories with a moral to them. We call these 'parables'. But Luke is far more interested in them than any other Gospel-writer. He alone tells the tale of the prodigal son for instance.

Only Matthew

3 Of the four Gospel-writers, only Matthew tells us of Jesus's Sermon on the Mount. No one else records Jesus's words about those who make peace.

Only Matthew and Luke

4 The 'Lord's prayer' is found only in the Gospels of Matthew and Luke — and even here the two writers give *different versions* of what Jesus said.

Only John

5 Only John's Gospel tells the story of Jesus turning water into wine.

Crucifixion

6 An account of Jesus's trial and death is to be found — set out in detail — in all four Gospels.

Resurrection

7 Matthew, Luke and John tell different stories of how Jesus appears to his followers after he had died on the cross. Mark has no story of this 'resurrection'.

These differences between the four Gospels, each supposedly setting out the most important events of Jesus's life, have puzzled men and women for centuries. So startled were some Christians that Mark never tells of Jesus appearing after death to his followers that they added extra sections to his Gospel, giving such appearances. (You can read them, set out in modern Bibles: Mark chapter 16, verse 9 onwards.)

Mark's puzzling omission

Some searching questions

So these seven items raise some interesting questions:

Early life   1 If Mark and John never mention the early life of Jesus, did they know nothing about these years?

Sermon on the   2 If only Matthew records the Sermon on the Mount, did it
Mount   really take place. Had the other three Gospel-writers never heard about it?

Prodigal son   3 Since neither Matthew, nor Mark nor John cared to include in his Gospel the famous story of the prodigal son, did Jesus really tell it, or did Luke (or one of his informants) make it up and put it into Jesus's mouth?

4 If the four Gospels differ so strikingly in the accounts they give of the life and teaching of Jesus, can we assume there
Gospel truth   is anything we can still call 'Gospel truth'?

Answers to these questions are not easy; but this book hopes to provide some.

To study the life and teaching of Jesus makes you work hard. Modern religious studies do not destroy people's faiths. But they can also interest those who do not have much faith.

Above all this study allows you to work out things for yourself. There are experiments which every person can do on his or her own behalf.

1 Two experiments

The first is to write out, side by side in separate columns, the
Lord's prayer   Lord's prayer as recorded in:

- Matthew chapter 6, verses 9 to 13;
- Luke chapter 11, verses 2 to 4.

What are the differences? Here are some suggestions:

1 Luke is shorter than Matthew in his account. Luke stresses that God's gifts (daily bread, etc.) never fail; they come to us each day. Matthew is more concerned to stress our instant needs ('Give us *this day* our daily bread').
2 Matthew is talking about a very special sort of 'evil' action:

The Crucifixion by Mathias Grünewald

being tempted by an evil being, some sort of devil. Luke speaks of any kind of evil temptation as something we need God's help to avoid.

3 Ask whether people over several years, using the same prayer, lengthen or shorten it. This will help us to decide which is closer to the original version — the Lord's prayer in Matthew, or the Lord's prayer in Luke.

An account of Jesus's life

A second experiment is to write out your own remembered account of the life and teaching of Jesus. Include the seven points mentioned above. Then compare it with the fuller story of his life that follows in this book.

2 A project on the crucifixion

Read the four accounts of the crucifixion of Jesus in:

- Matthew chapter 27, verses 32 to 54;
- Mark chapter 15, verses 21 to 39;
- Luke chapter 23, verses 26 to 47;
- John chapter 19, verses 17 to 30.

Make four separate lists of the events as they happen in the order described by these four Gospels. See where they differ and where they agree with each other. Questions to ask include:

> What did Jesus say on the cross — according to each Gospel?
> Who was present at the crucifixion — according to each Gospel?
> What image of Jesus is each Gospel especially wanting to present to us?

2 The Life and Teaching of Jesus more detail

A longer summary of the life and teaching of Jesus

1 The early years

Birth

Just before King Herod the Great died (in 4 BC) Jesus was born, probably in Bethlehem, though he lived as a child and young man in Nazareth where his father was a carpenter. His mother's name was Mary. Two Gospels say that Mary was a virgin when Jesus was born.

Baptism

In the year AD 27 (or shortly after that) Jesus's cousin John began to pour water from the river Jordan over those who wanted to be made clean of their sins. John (known as 'the Baptist') preached that a greater one then he would soon announce the coming of God's rule on earth. Jesus came to John and asked to be washed in the Jordan.

2 The three public years

Miracles
Stories

This baptism was the start of three years in which Jesus made an enormous public impact in this small part of the world. He preached. He performed miracles. He told stories. He chose twelve special followers, as well as another group, which numbered perhaps seventy people, ready to transmit all they had learned of and from Jesus to the rest of the world.

Disciples

Jesus announced what he called good news: that God's rule was about to happen. Jesus even seemed to say at times that he would be king when God's rule came. The twelve chief followers would be leaders in the new kingdom.

All this involved criticism of those who claimed to

Enemies

represent God. Some of the Jewish leaders therefore grew to hate Jesus. Also,he demanded that those who wanted to be part of the new kingdom of God should beg forgiveness for their sins and promise to lead a better life. Moreover, the idea of a new king, ruling in the land of the Jews, frightened the Romans who at that time dominated all this part of the world. Would this new king threaten their rule?

Worship

All his life Jesus behaved as a pious Jew. He paid money to the Jerusalem Temple and told his followers to do the same. He worshipped God according to the rules of the Jewish Bible (now known among Christians as the Old Testament). But he also held that some leading Jews had

Jesus Cleansing the Temple by Gustav Doré

forgotten the true spirit of belief in God. They forgot the needs of the poor, for instance; they cared more for outdated rules and regulations than for doing good.

Jesus's life and teaching was mostly carried out in Galilee, though he sometimes taught in the region known as Judea and several times visited Jerusalem. The last time he went to Jerusalem, probably in the year AD 30, he knew he was in great danger. He rode into the city on a donkey, welcomed by a crowd. Matthew's Gospel tells us he did this to fit in with some words of the prophet Zechariah: 'Tell the daughter of Zion, "Here is your king, who comes to you in gentleness, riding on an ass, riding on the foal of a beast of burden".' Jesus then went to the Temple and threw out those who were using it simply to make money.

Galilee and Jerusalem

3 The suffering servant

For some time he had been teaching his followers that one way of being God's servant was by suffering. This idea he took from the Old Testament, chiefly from Isaiah chapter 52, verse 13, to chapter 53, verse 12). Now he decided to eat a final meal with his closest followers. In this 'Last Supper', as we call it, he broke bread — declaring that his body was soon to be broken — and he poured out wine — declaring that his blood was soon to be poured out.

The Last Supper

Then Jesus was arrested. The Jews managed to persuade the Roman rulers to put him on trial. He was condemned to die; and after being cruelly tortured, was crucified, by Roman soldiers, almost certainly on 7 April, AD 30. His body was broken; his blood was shed.

On trial

Crucifixion

Three days later many of his followers were reporting that his grave was empty. Some went so far as to claim that he had shown himself to be alive again.

Resurrection

Check how much of this summary of the life and teaching of Jesus fits in with your own list of the events you remember of his life.

The shortest Gospel — Mark — summarised

You can set out Mark's Gospel in *nine* simple sections:

1 Jesus begins his work

The preaching of John the Baptist
Jesus is baptised
Jesus finds his first followers
Jesus shows his authority and heals the sick

2 Jesus argues with some Jews (known as 'Pharisees')

Can Jesus forgive sins?
Why does Jesus mingle with sinners?
Should Christians fast?
Jesus has new views about the Pharisees' rules (and especially about the Sabbath day)

3 Jesus teaches

The parable of the sower
Some parables about the kingdom of God

4 Jesus acts

Stilling a storm
Healing
Feeding the multitude
Making a blind man see

5 The turning point

Peter's confession
Jesus is transfigured

6 On the way to Jerrusalem

A quarrel about divorce
Rich men and heaven
Jesus talks of his coming death
James and John talk about God's kingdom
The blind beggar

7 Jerusalem

Jesus enters the city
The parable of the wicked tenants
Arguing about the resurrection
Jesus speaks of the greatest of the laws

8 The end approaches

Jesus is anointed
The Last Supper
Jesus is arrested
Trial before the high priest
Peter betrays Jesus
Trial before Pilate

9 Death and the empty tomb

Jesus dies on the cross
Jesus is buried
The women find an empty tomb

Anyone who reads Mark's Gospel will find that much is omitted from these nine sections. And if you go on to read the other three Gospels and compare them with Mark's life of Jesus, you will learn much more that Mark never mentions.

3 Essential Knowledge about the Four Gospels

How, when and why?

1 Thirty years ago

How would you write about a famous person who lived, say, thirty years ago?

1 You would probably try to track down those who had known him, to gather together their memories.
2 You would read all you could find about this person (who, we are assuming here, was a man).
3 You would give 'background material' — what was going on in the rest of the world during his life — but only where this fitted in with his own activities.
4 You would give your own views about this man — why you think people should be interested in reading about him.

If you could find any letters or writing of the man himself, you would certainly use these. The Gospel-writers could not do this with Jesus, since Jesus himself wrote nothing down (though we know he once wrote in the sand). But people were soon collecting lists of his sayings and stories. They also got together an account of how he had been put on trial and killed.

2 When were the Gospels written?

If they were written by those who had watched every part of the life of Jesus — 'eyewitnesses' we would call them — then they would have a very great authority.

This, however, is not the case with our four Gospels. They

were not written immediately after Jesus's life on earth came to an end — about the year AD 30. Let's take the four Gospel's in order of writing.

Mark's Gospel

Probably in Rome, about the year AD 70 a man named Mark wrote out the first of the four Gospels. So the first Gospel was written down *forty years after* the events it describes.

Another point: Mark was not apparently interested in writing down everything he could discover about Jesus. His aim was to tell the 'good news' about Jesus as he understood it. Some later Christians tell us that he learned much from one of Jesus's chief followers, Peter.

Luke's Gospel

About ten years later (maybe a little more than that) two other men set down their understanding of the 'good news' about Jesus. They were Matthew and Luke. Luke was a doctor of medicine. He was not a Jew. He was fascinated by the idea that the spirit of God and Jesus could fill people in his day. He wanted to show how the good news applied to the whole world, not just Jews. He loved stories of Jesus healing the sick.

Matthew's Gospel

Matthew by contrast wrote the good news, as he understood it, for Jews. A Jew himself,, he wanted to show that those Jews who had turned against Jesus had been mistaken.

Then a fourth Gospel was written, the Gospel according to John. Jesus had a follower who was very close to him, named John. (Mark, Luke and Matthew were not among the first followers of Jesus, even though one of his company was called Matthew.) Could it have been written by this man

John's Gospel

towards the end of a long life? His aim, he wrote, was to convince people that 'Jesus is the Christ, the son of God, and believing this, to have life in his name.' Later we shall try to show the chief characteristics of Mark, Luke, Matthew and John.

Briefly we should note here that John is very different from the other three Gospels. For one thing, although Jesus loved to teach in parables, John scarcely mentions this. Also, John has his own strange ways of describing Jesus — as, for example, the WORD OF GOD, or the I AM.

For these reasons some people have insisted that John's Gospel must have been written a very long time after the other three. This cannot be true, for we have discovered in the desert very early parchment copies of John's Gospel. We are nearly certain that it must have been written before the end of the first century AD. The writer claims to have been

Jesus's specially beloved disciple, and this may well be so.

But this is still a long time after the life of Jesus on earth. The long gap between Jesus's life and the Gospels that tell us about it accounts for many difficulties these Gospels give us. No one in a classroom, for example (except perhaps the teacher!) is likely to remember anything that happened forty years ago.

3 Why were the Gospels written?

The tales about Jesus were handed on in the early days of Christianity because men and women felt they could help them in their daily lives and because they needed to know who this Jesus was. They believed he had risen from death. They believed he was the son of God. All this made them look back on his life in a special way. Here was no mortal man, sinful, sometimes foolish like the rest of us. Here was a man who was still alive and active, even if in invisible ways; a man specially sent to show us the secret of eternal life. Yet he ended his life in disgrace, crucified as a criminal.

**Gospels
interpret**

Matthew, Mark, Luke and John all present this as the working out of God's own will. They do not wish to give us simple facts and let us draw our own conclusions. Always they *interpret* what is going on.

Throughout their Gospels, Mark, Matthew, Luke and John are insisting that by his life and teaching — and above all by his death and rising from death — Jesus taught us how to live and brought us eternal life. They do not wish to give us simple straightforward history. As John wrote towards the end of his Gospel, **'these things were written that you might believe that Jesus is the Christ, the son of God, and that believing you may have life in him.'**

So the Gospel-writers held that everything they wrote down about Jesus was of supreme importance to those who were about to read about him. Mark, Matthew, Luke and John believed passionately in what they were writing. This passion colours their Gospels.

The characters of the Gospel-writers

Even when a man or woman writes a novel simply to entertain readers, that novel reveals the character of the

Characters of today's writers

author. Some of the best-sellers of the twentieth century are written by people who must have been fascinated by violence and brutality, since the novels themselves are full of this. Other 'soap-operas' are filled with sentimental romance and old-fashioned cosiness; again, this reflects the authors' values as well as being calculated to appeal widely.

1 Special interests and the order of events

Reading the four Gospels, we can spot the special interests of each writer. There is much more about this in Chapter 4 which follows. Special interests affected the way the Gospel-writers set out their story. An early writer (the church historian Eusebius) tells us that Mark 'interpreted Peter and carefully wrote down what Jesus did and said, though not in order.' All four Gospel-writers changed the order in which they tell the story of Jesus, according to their own special interests.

Variety in order of events

There's nothing strange about this. Suppose you come back from holiday with a set of photographs. How do you set them out in an album or to show to friends? You can, if you wish, simply show each photo in the order it was taken. But most of us arrange them by topics.

Holiday photographs

Topic 1: this is me and my boyfriend on the beach;
this is my uncle Albert on the beach;
this is Johnnie gingerly putting a toe into the sea;
this is mother diving from the rocks.
Topic 2: this is me and my boyfriend at a night-club;
this is uncle Albert trying to dance;
this is Johnnie trying to order some food;
this is mother driving us home from the night-club.
Topic 3: this is me and my boyfriend at the fair;
this is uncle Albert on the swings. . . .
and so on.

2 Special interests — an example from Matthew's Gospel

The Gospels do exactly the same with their pictures of Jesus. Matthew, for example, gathers together some vital sentences

Sermon on the Mount
of Jesus about *happiness* and calls these 'the Sermon on the Mount'. No other Gospel-writer does this. This is one of Matthew's special topics.

3 Different ways of arranging the material

Sometimes three Gospels arrange their material in one way and a fourth disagrees. So Matthew, Mark and Luke tell how Jesus threw out of the Temple those who were using it as a market place. They place this story just before that of Jesus being caught by his enemies and put on trial. John's Gospel puts the same incident almost at the very beginning of Jesus's public life and teaching. He goes up to Jerusalem and finds in the Temple people selling oxen and sheep and pigeons, as well as others changing money. Making a whip of cords,

Cleansing of the Temple
Jesus drives them all out, overturning the tables of the money-changers and pouring their cash on to the ground. From the very start of Jesus's public ministry, John wants to say, he challenged the corrupt ways that had invaded God's house. This 'topic' was so important for John that he brought it to the forefront of his Gospel, whereas the other three Gospel-writers leave it till the very end of his active life.

So we come back to our first attempt to write an account of the life of Jesus. With the information at our disposal it is impossible. Of course the Gospels all agree on many events in his public life and teaching; but their writers simply did not care about a simple history — beginning at the birth of Jesus and going on till the end of his life on earth.

4 Special interests — an example from Luke's Gospel

Luke on prayer
To give one final example of how we learn about the Gospel-writers themselves from what they wrote, Luke was more fascinated by prayer than any of the other three. Luke — like Matthew and Mark — tells that Jesus chose twelve chief followers. All three Gospel-writers give the names of these twelve men. But only Luke begins his account with the words, Jesus 'went out to the mountain to pray; and he continued in prayer to God throughout the whole night.'

Clearly Luke believed that whenever Jesus made such a great decision he needed to pray. Even more: Luke wants those who read his Gospel to know that before any important decision, we too should pray to God.

No doubt the other three Gospel-writers believed in prayer too; but they never stress it so much as Luke.

4 The Four Gospels

Matthew

1 One of the twelve disciples?

Matthew clearly longed to persuade Jews to accept the teachings of Jesus and to agree that Jesus was the long-expected king of the Jews. He wrote as a Christian Jew for his fellow-Jews. A very early tradition says that this Gospel-writer was one of Jesus's twelve closest apostles — a former tax-collector who lived in Capernaum — and that the Gospel was written in Aramaic (which was Jesus's own language).

Aramaic or Greek?

If this is so, our present Gospel is a translation of this Aramaic original, since it has come down to us in Greek. This is something we simply cannot be sure about. If, as most modern scholars believe, Matthew copied part of his Gospel from Mark, it is hard to accept that he was one of the twelve disciples. Why should a man who had been with Jesus almost from the beginning use the evidence of a writer who had never seen Jesus face-to-face? So we can't be certain who Matthew was.

2 Defending Christianity

The church

We can see that he committed himself strongly to the early church. Since some Jews at this time had turned against the Christians, Matthew seems to have longed for an equally strong organisation to defend Christianity against those who were increasingly attacking it. (Chapter 18 of Matthew's Gospel sets out rules for dealing with a fellow-Christian who is straying. The section Matthew chapter 18, verses 15 to 20 is one of only two in the four Gospels which actually uses the

St Matthew
from Butler's
*Lives of the
Saints*

**Organised
church**

word *church.* The other is two chapters earlier — in the
section Matthew chapter 16, verses 13 to 20. Both these
sections can be read to give the flavour of Matthew's
thinking.) He wants a morally stern church, with a properly
agreed organisation. At the same time he wishes Christians
to treat each other with great gentleness, even when one has
offended another. And he finds suitable stories from the life
of Jesus to support his attitude.

3 The Old Testament prophecies fulfilled

In his desire to convince the Jews that Jesus is the promised saviour as proclaimed in the Old Testament, Matthew refers to the Old Testament more than 130 times and explicitly quotes it 43 times. Many events which seem to happen by chance are explained by Matthew as mysteriously developing out of something predicted in the Old Testament (for example, when the enemies of Jesus — seeing that their ally, the former disciple Judas, has hanged himself — take back their bribe of thirty pieces of silver, Matthew in chapter 27, verses 9 and 10, says they used the money to bring about a prophecy of the Old Testament writer Jeremiah). For Matthew, the Old Testament foretells the New.

> **Writing for fellow Jews**

> **Old Testament**

Matthew's close concern with the Old Testament becomes extremely important when he sets about showing who Jesus really was. A good many Jews at this time were looking for a Messiah (the Hebrew equivalent of the Greek word 'Christ') who would take on the Romans in battle on their behalf. They wanted a political leader. Matthew continually insists that Jesus is come as ruler of the *kingdom of heaven*. He records many parables in which Jesus describes what this kingdom of heaven is like (see, for example, chapter 20, verses 1 to 16, and chapter 22, verses 1 to 14). But when his disciple Peter wishes to fight to defend Jesus against those who come to capture him, Jesus makes him put his sword away. Matthew has Jesus insist that what is happening, including his arrest and imminent death, is all to fulfil the Old Testament prophecies.

> **Jews wanted political leader**

4 Matthew writes like a Jewish rabbi

The rabbis taught often by suggesting groups of ideas — in threes or sevens — and so does Matthew. He even presents Jesus as a teacher, gathering together five great lessons, each one in the form of a powerful lecture:

> **Patterns**

1 The Sermon on the Mount (chapters 5 to 7)
2 Teaching for the disciples who are to go to preach to others (chapter 10)
3 Teaching by means of seven parables about the kingdom of heaven (chapter 13, verses 1 to 52)
4 Teaching about the rules for the church (chapter 18)

5 Teaching about the final coming of the kingdom of heaven (chapters 24 and 25)

Matthew also loved patterns in his writing. Consider the name he gives to Jesus in his first chapter (verse 23): Emmanuel, which means *God with us.* For twenty-eight more chapters Matthew never refers explicitly to the idea that Jesus brings God to us. Then, in the very last verse of his Gospel he quotes Jesus as saying. 'Lo, I am *with you always,* to the end of the world.'

Not surprisingly, we can spot such a pattern running through the whole of Matthew's Gospel. A prologue reveals the mystery of Jesus (chapters 1 and 2). Why do three mysterious wise men from the east bring gifts to an obscure baby in Bethlehem? How can such a baby, born of a virgin, be descended from Abraham, the father of the Jews?

Seven stages   In seven stages, the rest of the Gospel answers these questions:

1 God announces that this baby is his son — a son whom Satan fails to corrupt (chapters 3 and 4).
2 Jesus, by miracles which follow his Sermon on the Mount, himself announces that God's kingdom has arrived (chapters 5 to 9).
3 First Jesus's disciples and then Jesus himself announce to the Jewish world the good news of the kingdom (chapters 10 to 12); Jesus himself is bringing that kingdom to men and women on earth.
4 Men and women must respond to all this: do they accept that Jesus is the son of God and the longed-for successor of Abraham? Jesus speaks of this in seven parables and then Peter, his chief disciple, declares that Jesus is 'the Christ, the son of the living God'. Jesus now describes Peter as the first of all those who shall follow him (chapter 13 to chapter 16, verse 20).
5 Jesus teaches his disciples about suffering as the way to bring about his kingdom. He proclaims his own death (chapter 16, verse 21, to the end of chapter 17).
6 The kingdom of God is revealed as the church (chapters 18 to 23).
7 Jesus decisively brings into being the kingdom of heaven by submitting himself to death at the hands of wicked men

and women. After rising from death, he commands his disciples to persuade men and women throughout the world to follow him (chapters 24 to 28).

1 The story of the wise men worshipping the infant Jesus is found only in .... Gospel.
2 The Lord's Prayer is found only in the Gospels of .... and ....
3 Only the Gospel of .... sets out Jesus's Sermon on the Mount.
4 Give three examples of how Matthew in his Gospel tried to persuade the Jews to accept the teachings of Jesus.
5 Using three examples, illustrate how Matthew tried to convince the Jews that Jesus was the promised saviour as proclaimed in the Old Testament.
6 Make a plan, setting out the stages of Matthew's Gospel.

Mark

1 An exciting story

Powerful writing

Mark's Gospel, as a British scholar (William Neil) once observed, 'has a notably staccato effect. Few words are wasted.' He starts off immediately by presenting his readers with what he regards as the most important information they shall ever be given. The very first verse of the Gospel describes Jesus as the Christ, the son of God, adding that this is the start of good news for mankind.

This staccato effect continues throughout the whole Gospel. As a result Mark is an exciting read, a fast read (and sometimes a frightening read). Mark is a brilliant story-teller. In a few words he can sum up a character and what that person is feeling. (Read, for example, in Mark chapter 5, verses 25 to 34, the story of the woman too scared to ask Jesus to cure her illness. Imagine all the different emotions she feels in such a short time.)

Everything moves at a sparkling pace in Mark. His is the shortest of the four Gospels. He does not bother to give many details of how times passes. He tells us that Jesus did something 'immediately' or 'after some days'. Mark does not expect his readers to care how much time elapsed between the extraordinary things Jesus did and said.

2 Where did Mark obtain his information?

He did not get it from the other Gospels, since his was written first. About the year AD 135 a writer named Papias asserted that Mark was the interpreter of Jesus's leading disciple Peter. This could very well be true. In the Acts of the Apostles we read about a Mark whose mother had a house in Jerusalem used by the first Christians, including Peter. The first letter of Peter also describes a certain Mark as a loving friend.

Peter's interpreter?

Peter probably was crucified in Rome, and Mark's Gospel certainly betrays a Roman origin. Writing for a non-Jewish community, he translates Jewish words; but he also translates Roman terms, since his readers were Greeks. So, as well as the stories Peter told him, Mark could also draw on the memories of Christians in Rome who had learned about Jesus (or even known him).

Roman Christians as source

In addition Mark drew on stories about Jesus already written down. We can see this because he sometimes tells the same story twice. Look at the following two sequences side by side.

Written sources

Mark chapter 6, verse 34, to chapter 7, verse 37:	Mark chapter 8, verses 1 to 26:
Jesus feeds five thousand people	Jesus feeds four thousand people
(Jesus walks on water)	
Jesus crosses a lake	Jesus crosses a lake
Jesus argues with Pharisees	Jesus argues with Pharisees
(Jesus meets a Syro-Phoenician woman)	
Jesus heals a deaf-mute	Jesus heals a blind man

Here is the same sequence of events in Jesus's life, used twice by Mark. He must have found them already written down in two separate documents and incorporated both in his Gospel.

THE FOUR GOSPELS 23

3 The first Gospel

Taking all these elements:

> Peter's memories,
> stories about Jesus learned from others,
> written sources,

Mark wove them into the first Gospel of the Christian church.
If we study chapter 13 we can guess almost exactly *when* he
wrote. Between AD 66 and 70 Jewish heroes took to the hills
and began to fight against their Roman masters. In AD 70 the
Romans destroyed the Jerusalem Temple.

Mark makes Jesus foresee all this. Perhaps Jesus did
foresee it; but Mark's detailed descriptions of the horrors of
the Jewish wars and the destruction of the Temple suggest
that he knew exactly what had happened. (Read especially
chapter 13, verse 14: 'But when you see the desolating
sacrilege set up where it ought not to be (let the reader
understand), then let those who are in Judea flee to the

**Written around
AD 70**

mountains.') So we assume that Mark wrote this first Gospel
around the year AD 70, since he refers to events happening
then.

The other three Gospels are longer than Mark's. He omits:
at the beginning, any account of Jesus as a baby or young
man; *at the end,* any account of an appearance of the risen
Jesus to his followers.

**No
appearance of
risen Christ**

This is very startling — until one realises that Mark puts
the first followers of Jesus into our own position: they have to
believe in the resurrection of Jesus without having seen him
bodily. A Gallup Poll in 1984 asked members of the Church
of England the following:

> 'Some people have believed and still believe, that Jesus
> was raised bodily from the dead, three days after his
> crucifixion. Others have suggested that after the crucifixion
> Jesus was not raised bodily from the dead, but made his
> personality and presence known to his disciples in a
> spiritual but not bodily way. Which if either of these two
> views comes closest to your own, or have you got no views
> on these topics?'

No more than 52 per cent of Anglican lay members said they
believed Jesus rose bodily from the dead. Nearly a third
replied that in their view Jesus was not raised bodily, but

made his personality and presence known to his disciples only spiritually.

Clearly some Christians do not need believe in a bodily resurrection. Mark's Gospel gives us no evidence that there was one.

4 Mark has several special themes

He emphasises these themes throughout his Gospel. First he wrestles with the question: why did people not recognise that Jesus was the Christ, the Messiah? He decides that Jesus deliberately concealed the truth from people who were not worthy to receive it. When Jesus spoke in parables, Mark says this was not to open people's eyes to a new truth. The parables were spoken to *conceal* the truth from the foolish. Only those who were closest to Jesus could understand them. And when in Mark chapter 8 Peter declares that he believes Jesus to be the Christ, Jesus orders his disciples to tell **Messianic** nobody this. We call all this deliberate concealment of the **secret** truth about Jesus the Messianic secret.

Next Mark asks why Jesus should have suffered so much. God sent him to save men and women from their fears, their faults, their sins. Did it all go wrong? Mark tries to show that God often uses apparent failure to produce wonderful results. The prophet Isaiah (in chapter 53) wrote of a servant of God who would be despised and rejected by **The suffering** men. Mark sees Jesus as such a suffering servant. In chapter **servant** 8 he tells us that Jesus began to teach his disciples 'that the son of man must suffer many things, and be rejected by the elders and the chief priests and the scribes, and be killed, and after three days rise again'.

Mark also knew that Christians in his day were suffering persecution. The Emperor Nero had killed many of them. Mark showed how Jesus had suffered in his day just as Christians were now suffering. He reminded Christians that Jesus warned them they would suffer too. He also wrote down Jesus's promises that those who were willing to put up with such treatment would find their reward in heaven. (Read on this Mark chapter 8, verses 34 to 38, and chapter 10, verses 28 to 30.)

1 Write down the name of the Gospel which, in the opinion of most scholars, was the first to be written. What is its approximate date?

2 One Gospel-writer claimed to be the specially beloved disciple of Jesus. Who was he?

3 The Sermon on the Mount is to be found in .... Gospel. (Write down the Gospel's name.)

4 Why do the writers of the four Gospels not present their accounts of the life and teaching of Jesus in the same order?

5 Which Gospel-writer was fascinated by prayer?

6 Write down five points you have learned about Matthew.

7 Make a plan which sets out the stages of Matthew's Gospel.

8 Which is the shortest of the four Gospels?

9 Mark sometimes tells the same story twice, though in slightly different ways. Give three examples of this.

10 The other three Gospels are longer than Mark's. What important parts of the life and teaching of Jesus does Mark omit?

11 Mark was brilliant at telling stories. Illustrate the truth of this, using three stories from his Gospel.

12 What did Mark write about:
   1 parables?
   2 why Jesus suffered?
   3 why people failed to spot that Jesus claimed to be the Christ?

Luke

1 The Greek companion of the Apostle Paul

Best educated Gospel-writer

Luke, whose Gospel stands third in the books of our present New Testament, was the best educated, most cultivated of the four Gospel-writers. He is also the only writer of a New Testament book who was not a Jew.

Luke was a Greek. He was a companion of Paul the Apostle on several missionary journeys, and he wrote about these as well as writing his Gospel. The Acts of the Apostles, his second book, in fact follows immediately on the Gospel, taking up the story after Jesus had ascended to heaven. Many New Testament writers faced up to the problem that

imago   ui   uiy

AGIOS

LUCAS

St Luke from
the *Lindisfarne
Gospels*

while the earliest Christians had expected Jesus to come
back again almost immediately, this didn't happen. Luke
believed that in a sense he *had* come back. His Holy Spirit
inspired his followers, showed them what to do,
strengthened them in any difficulty or disaster. Luke's Gospel
Interest in the is far more interested in the work of this Holy Spirit (which is
Holy Spirit God's spirit as well as Jesus's) than are Matthew, Mark or
John. The Holy Spirit, he says, 'came upon' the Virgin Mary
when she conceived Jesus. John the Baptist's mother
Elizabeth was 'filled with the Holy Spirit'. Eventually (in his
Acts of the Apostles), after Jesus had gone to heaven all his

disciples sat together in a room in Jerusalem and 'were all filled with the Holy Spirit'. The Holy Spirit, in Luke's view, continued Jesus's work on earth.

Doctor

St Paul, in his letter to the Colossians, calls Luke the beloved doctor. There is an entertaining confirmation of this in his Gospel. We have already looked at Mark's story of a woman who was healed by touching the hem of Jesus's clothing (Mark chapter 5, verses 25 to 34). Mark says she 'had suffered a great deal under many doctors, and had spent all her money on them, and was no better but rather grew worse'. Luke tells all this story, which he copies from Mark; but he obviously did not like this criticism of his own profession, and at this point all he says is that the woman had suffered for twelve years 'and could not be healed by anyone' (Luke chapter 8, verses 43 to 48).

2 The historian

Curiously enough, unlike Matthew, Mark and John, Luke does not claim to be writing a 'Gospel', that is giving the 'good news' about Jesus. He sets out instead to be an historian. Like other historians of his time, he dedicates his book to an important person (Luke calls him 'most excellent Theophilus'; Theophilus means 'lover of God'). At the beginning of his Gospel, Luke writes that he knows many others have compiled a 'narrative' of what has happened in Palestine as a result of the coming of Jesus. They have done so using the evidence of those who saw it for themselves. Now Luke says he wishes to do the same.

Concern for facts and dates

Again and again he mentions what is happening in world affairs, in order to date what Jesus did. John the Baptist began to teach and preach, he says:

1 when Tiberius Caesar had reigned for fifteen years;
2 when Pontius Pilate was governor of Judea;
3 when Herod ruled in Galilee;
4 when Herod's brother Philip ruled in the region of Ituraea and Trachonitis;
5 when Lysanias ruled over Abilene;
6 when Annas and Caiaphas were high priests in Jerusalem.
(Luke chapter 3, verses 1 to 2)

Here is a Gospel-writer extremely careful that his facts and dates are correct.

3 A Gospel for all people

A non-Jewish view

As a non-Jew Luke wants to stress that Jesus came for the whole world, not just for his own people. He likes to quote words of Jesus which praise non-Jews (read chapter 4, verses 25 to 27). At the end of his Gospel Luke tells us that Jesus said that 'repentance and forgiveness should be preached to all the nations, beginning in Jerusalem'. So his is a Gospel for all people.

Concern for downtrodden

It is also a Gospel for the downtrodden and the outcast. In Jesus's time shepherds were considered very lowly people. It is no accident that whereas Matthew tells us about wise men from the east who came to worship the infant Jesus, in Luke these are replaced by shepherds — the first to hear that the saviour has been born.

Shepherds replace wise men

Concern for women

Women too in Jesus's time were often despised. Luke makes a special effort to show their devotion to Jesus and Jesus's care for them. The sinner Mary Magdalene; a widow who could scarcely find enough money to pay the Temple collection; Martha and Mary, the sisters of Lazarus; women who come to Jesus's tomb: all these are painted with great tenderness by Luke.

Concern for poor

His Gospel is also, he writes, one addressed to the poor. Mary, learning that she is to be the mother of Jesus, sings a song in Luke, chapter 1, which proclaims:

God 'has put down the mighty from their seats,
and exalted those of low degree;
he has filled the hungry with good things,
and the rich he has sent empty away.'

The Holy Spirit anoints Jesus 'to preach good news to the poor' (Luke chapter 4, verse 18). Jesus tells John the Baptist that he is preaching 'good news to the poor'.

This love for the poor is found in parables recorded by Luke. Read chapter 14, verses 7 to 14. The conclusion of this parable is:

'When you give a dinner or a banquet, do not invite your friends or your brothers or your kinsmen or your rich neighbours, in the hope that they will invite you in return and you will be repaid. Instead, when you give a feast, invite the poor, the maimed, the lame, the blind, and you will be blessed, because they cannot repay you. You will be repaid at the resurrection of the just.'

The rich man and poor Lazarus

Below: Christ in the house of Martha and Mary by Jan Vermeer

Luke alone tells Jesus's parable of the rich man and poor Lazarus (chapter 16, verses 19 to 31). Lazarus lies outside the gates of the rich man's dwelling. He is covered in ulcerating sores. All he has to eat are crumbs which fall from the rich man's table. The rich man never notices him until — after death and tormented in hell — he sees poor Lazarus, now in paradise, comforted by Abraham. Luke stresses that we cannot be the friend of God and at the same time love material things. The poor have no such temptations. The poor, Luke says (quoting Jesus), are blessed.

4 The five stages of the Gospel

Five stages

As with Matthew (pages 19–20) and Mark (pages 9–10), we can make a plan setting out the various stages of Luke's Gospel. The Gospel falls into five parts:

1 A short introduction, saying why Luke wrote his Gospel and how he found his sources (chapter 1, verses 1 to 4)
2 The birth and boyhood of Jesus (chapter 1, verse 5, to chapter 2, verse 52. NB no other Gospel-writer tells us about Jesus as a boy)
3 Jesus in Galilee (chapter 4, verse 14, to chapter 9, verse 50. NB this includes the Sermon on the Plain — Luke's equivalent of Matthew's Sermon on the Mount)
4 Jesus teaches about the kingdom of God (chapter 9, verse 51, to chapter 18, verse 30)
5 Holy Week — the last eight days of Jesus's life on earth (chapter 18, verse 31, to chapter 24, verse 53)

Acts continues the story

Remember, however, that Luke's story does not end here. The history he is recounting continues in the Acts of the Apostles. Here Luke tells us that Jesus, after his resurrection, spent another forty days with his disciples, before ascending into heaven.

5 Luke's special teaching

4 parables only in Luke

Section 4 of the plan above contains Luke's special teaching. Other sections of his Gospel, as we have seen, have their own special traits. But in the nine or so chapters that form section 4 Luke tells us much about Jesus's teaching that is not stressed elsewhere in the Gospels. The section contains, for instance, four parables found only in Luke's Gospel:

1 The parable of the good Samaritan
Jesus here transforms the notion of a 'neighbour'. This parable reveals Jesus ignoring any barriers of race or belief, in the interests of simply doing good to a person in need.

(Luke chapter 10, verses 30 to 37)

2 The parable of the prodigal son
Luke's special material tells us that Jesus believed there
was more joy in heaven when one wayward person came
to his senses than over ninety-nine 'good' people, who
looked down on the sinner because they had never fallen
into such straits.

(Luke chapter 15, verses 11 to 32)

3 The parable of the rich man and Lazarus
This shows God's attitude to the selfish rich and to the
poor.

(Luke chapter 16, verses 19 to 31)

4 The parable of the Pharisee and the tax collector
Another parable told by Jesus (Luke says) 'to some who
trusted in themselves and despised others'. The Pharisee
prays in the Temple simply to praise himself — foolishly to
tell God how good his servant has been. The tax collector
can think of nothing to say in defence of himself. The
conclusion of the parable is that the tax collector leaves the
Temple in greater favour with God than the Pharisee, 'for
(Jesus said) every one who exalts himself will be humbled,
but whoever humbles himself will be exalted.'

(Luke chapter 18, verses 9 to 14)

6 The compassionate Gospel

Luke's Gospel, then, is a humane one. He presents an
extremely compassionate Jesus. A tiny parable, found only in
Luke, emphasises Jesus's care for the lost sinner, the person
who has gone astray, whom God still loves and wishes to
reclaim:

Jesus's care for lost sinners

'Is there a woman who possesses ten silver coins, loses
one and does not light a lamp and sweep everywhere in
her house and look with the utmost care until she finds it?
When she has found it, she calls all her friends and
neighbours together and cries, "Be happy with me: I have
found the coin I had lost." Just so, I tell you, the angels of
God rejoice over one sinner who repents.'

(Luke chapter 15, verses 8 to 10)

Enemies of Jesus

Jesus, Luke says, told this parable when the Pharisees and
scribes were criticising him for showing friendship to sinners
and even eating with them. Of course his words greatly
angered them. Shortly after this section of Luke's Gospel we
are not surprised to read (chapter 19, verse 47) that 'the chief

priests and the scribes sought to destroy him'. At that
moment the people who loved Jesus prevented this. But soon
his enemies succeeded in crucifying him.

1 Luke was a .... and a companion of
   .... on several missionary journeys. (Fill in the
   missing words.)
2 Give two reasons why we think that Luke was a doctor of
   medicine.
3 As a historian Luke was especially interested in world
   affairs at the time of Jesus. Give three examples of this
   interest, taken from his Gospel.
4 In his writings, Luke shows women as especially devoted
   to Jesus. Give two examples of this.
5 Tell one story showing Luke's attitude to prayer.
6 Luke's Gospel falls into five parts. Name them.
7 Luke presents a Jesus designed to appeal to non-Jewish
   readers. Illustrate this statement by using three examples
   from his Gospel.

John

1 When was it written?

John's Gospel is so different from the other three Gospels of
the Bible that for many years scholars assumed that it must
have been written many many years later. Twentieth-century
discoveries proved them wrong.

In 1935 an ancient fragment of the Gospel was published.
It is now in the John Rylands Library, Manchester. Although
it only contains tiny sections of John's Gospel (on one side
chapter 18, verses 31 to 33; on the other side chapter 18,
verses 37 and 38), undoubtedly this is part of the whole
Gospel. Scientists can without any doubt date this fragment
around the year AD 150, if not slightly earlier. The fragment
was found in Egypt. So we must conclude that if a Gospel
about events in Palestine could have reached Egypt by 150
AD at the latest, it must have been written maybe even fifty
years earlier. John's Gospel, we now think, was written
between AD 90 and 100.

**Fragment
found**

Another reason — alongside the evidence of this early fragment from Egypt — has been offered to support the notion that John's Gospel was written before the end of the first century AD. Some passages in the Gospel — which we now have in Greek — are quite obscure. They make sense if we see them as an imperfect translation from Aramaic. If the Gospel was first written in Aramaic and then translated into Greek, that must have been quite early in the history of Christianity: for Greek soon became the language of every Christian writing.

More evidence for early date

2 Different from the other Gospels

Spiritual Gospel

Yet John is still very different from the other three Gospels. Eusebius called it a spiritual Gospel. He meant that, while the other three give the physical events of Jesus's life, John shows their hidden meaning. This is unfair to Matthew, Mark and Luke. All three want to show the hidden depths of Jesus's life and teaching. But John does explicitly state (chapter 16, verses 12 and 13) that Jesus had many things to tell his disciples that they were not yet ready for. The Holy Spirit would teach them these things. John clearly implies

Below: A fragment of St John's Gospel

**New
revelations**

that he is now telling his readers some of these new
revelations.

**Long
discourses**

John is notable for long discourses by Jesus, none of which
are found in any other Gospel. Indeed, nothing like them is
found in any other Gospel. You can read these discourses in
the following sections of John's Gospel:

1 Chapter 13, verse 31, to chapter 14, verse 31, where Jesus
   tells his disciples about his own 'glorification' and about the
   Holy Spirit
2 Chapters 15 to 17, where Jesus talks about how we
   should live in his love and where he prays for his disciples

It is of course possible that Jesus spoke to his disciples in
these ways. But how did John write them down seventy or
more years later? Was anyone sitting at Jesus's feet taking it
all down? This seems unlikely.

Perhaps these are John's own meditations on the life and
teaching of Jesus. They contain some of the most remarkable
sayings of Jesus:

'Do not let your hearts be troubled; believe in God,
believe also in me. In my father's house are many rooms. If
this were not true, would I have told you that I go to
prepare a place for you?'

'I am the way, the truth and the life. No one comes to the
father but by me.'

'I am the vine; you are the branches. Live in me and I will
live in you.'

'This is my commandment: that you love one another as I
have loved you. Greater love has no man than this, that a
man lay down his life for his friends.'

I am

Notice how some of these sayings begin with the words 'I
am'. John knew that in the Old Testament is the story of God
revealing his name to Moses. God said to Moses: 'I AM WHO
I AM', God also said to Moses, 'say this to the people of
Israel, "I AM has sent me to you."'

It is a deliberate identification with God when John tells us
that Jesus says 'I am'. Jesus is showing us — through himself
— more of God's character. He is really claiming to be akin

to God. He says: 'Before Abraham was, I am,' (chapter 8, verse 58); and (two chapters later), 'I and the father are one.'

But we still have to ask: did Jesus really say these things? Nothing like them occurs in the other three Gospels.

3 The poet

Many Christians have decided that John was a kind of poet. A poet, looking back on the life of someone he or she loved, uses heightened language to describe that person. Walter de la Mare once wrote an epitaph on a beautiful lady:

Heightened language

> Here lies a most beautiful lady:
> Light of step and heart was she;
> I think she was the most beautiful lady
> That ever was in the West Country.

Now many other equally beautiful ladies must once have lived in the West Country. Walter de la Mare knew that with part of his mind. But his special lady was, to him, more beautiful than any other. He is not misleading us to say so.

Secondly, the poet pretends that his epitaph is found on a real tombstone. The poem has four more lines:

> But beauty vanishes; beauty passes;
> However rare — rare it be;
> And when I crumble, who will remember
> This lady of the West Country?

Again, Walter de la Mare is not tricking anybody by writing about an imaginary gravestone. He is not lying. He is writing poetry.

The idea of a gravestone crumbling (as human beings also crumble into dust when they die) expresses all he wants to say about how even the most beautiful people die and can be forgotten. This is the best way he can think of to bring home this truth to us. The gravestone is a poetic image.

Poetic images

John, writing about Jesus, uses poetic images like this. In John's Gospel we find Jesus using these images about himself. Jesus says:

> 'I am the light of the world'
> 'I am the bread of life'
> 'I am the good shepherd'
> 'I am the door for the sheep'
> 'I am the true vine'

Now we know that Jesus was not a shepherd, for instance. He was a carpenter. Obviously he wasn't a door, or a light, or a vine or bread.

But John, in writing these words down, is not tricking us or having Jesus tell lies. These are all poetic images. They are the best way John can find of bringing home to us who Jesus was.

Let us briefly look at two of them. First, in chapter 10, Jesus talks of the dangers to sheep — from robbers, from wolves, from shepherds who don't care about looking after the sheep. So sheep need to know where they can rest in safety. Jesus suggests that he can lead them to safety:

'I am the door,' he says; 'if anyone enters by me, he will go in and out and find pasture.'

(chapter 10, verse 9)

Next, sheep need a shepherd they can trust, someone who loves sheep, not someone who will let them stray and who is doing the work just for the pay.

Below: The Good Shepherd, a mosaic in Ravenna, Italy

'I am the good shepherd. The good shepherd lays down his life for the sheep.'

(chapter 10, verse 11)

All we need to ask now is 'Who are the sheep?' Is the answer 'Lost human beings, in search of a leader they can trust'?

4 Who was John?

The beloved disciple

Who would dare present this wholly original picture of Jesus? The author of this fourth Gospel describes himself as 'the disciple whom Jesus loved.' At the Last Supper Jesus's disciple John lay closest to him. This man was the brother of a disciple called James. He worked with Peter and Andrew, two of the first disciples chosen by Jesus. Jesus had a nickname for John and James: 'the sons of thunder'. One so close to his master might have dared put words into Jesus's mouth.

John at Ephesus

Early in the second century AD a bishop of Ephesus wrote that John, the beloved disciple, lay buried at Ephesus in Asia Minor. This could give us a clue about where the Gospel was written. About fifty years later Irenaeus, who was Bishop of Lyons in France, definitely stated that John wrote this Gospel at Ephesus.

But none of this really affects the fact that here we can read one of the most original minds ever to brood about and then write about the life and teaching of Jesus. Towards the end of his life a brilliant theologian (C H Dodd) declared:

> 'the gospel is so original and creative that a search for its "sources" or even for the "influences" by which it may have been affected, may easily lead us astray. Whatever influences may have been present have been masterfully controlled by a powerful and independent mind. There is no book, either in the New Testament or outside it, which is really *like* the Fourth Gospel.'
> (*The Interpretation of the Fourth Gospel*, Cambridge University Press)

5 The seven miracle-signs

Seven signs

As with the other three Gospels, we can make a plan of John's. He bases his Gospel on seven miracles of Jesus. But — very significantly — he does not call them miracles. For John they are all *signs*.

A signpost points towards something. If you are in Devonshire and come across a signpost with the name of (say) 'Totnes', you know you haven't reached that town. The signpost points you towards Totnes.

Now John did not agree with people who simply wanted to see miracles and marvel at them. He wanted us to see where Jesus's miracles were pointing. At a wedding the guests ran out of wine. Jesus turned water into wine for them. John says, 'Jesus did this, his first sign, at Cana in Galilee, and showed his glory; and his disciples believed in him.' (chapter 2, verse 11)

Water into wine

Not everyone saw where the sign of turning water into wine was pointing. Only his disciples understood. Jesus was 'showing his glory'. He was also making wonderful the most ordinary things: turning water into wine, and ordinary people into saints.

The other six miracle-signs in John's Gospel are:

1 Healing a sick boy (chapter 4, verses 46 to 54). Verse 54 reads: 'This was the second sign that Jesus did, when he had left Judea and come into Galilee.'
2 Feeding five thousand people (chapter 6, verses 1 to 14)
3 Walking on water (chapter 6, verses 16 to 21)
4 Healing a blind man (chapter 9, verses 1 to 7). In the previous chapter Jesus says, 'I am the light of the world,' and this sign points to this claim.
5 Jesus raises Lazarus from death (chapter 11, verses 1 to 44). In verse 25 Jesus says 'I am resurrection and life.' Again the sign points to this claim.
6 Jesus himself is raised from death (chapter 20 and chapter 21).

6 'I am the bread of life'

The Eucharist

John has another special interest — found in the other three Gospels but very much dwelt on in his: the Eucharist (or Holy Communion). As we shall see, Jesus at his last meal on earth with the disciples before his crucifixion told them to continue meeting together to break bread and share wine, in memory of him. Of the bread he said, 'This is my body,' of the wine he said, 'This is my blood'.

The Last Supper

You can read this story of the Last Supper in the other three Gospels (or in Paul's first letter to the Corinthians, chapter 11, verses 23 to 26). John does not tell us the story. He assumed that all of his readers knew it, and that they met each week for what they called the Eucharist, that is, to share this bread and wine.

Another sign

For John this meal is another kind of sign, pointing to what Jesus means for us. John seems to have the meal in his mind nearly all through his Gospel, and especially when Jesus fed five thousand people at once. At that time, according to John, Jesus spoke about being 'the bread of life'. He said:

Feeding the 5000

> 'I am the living bread which came down from heaven. If anyone eats this bread, he will live for ever. The bread which I shall give for the life of the world is my flesh.'
>
> (chapter 6, verse 51)

The Eucharist points to Jesus as the bread of life. Jesus promises to give us eternal life. But he knows he is going to be crucified first.

All this John puts into the poetic image, 'I am the bread of life'.

1 Fill in the word missing from this quotation:

'This deed at Cana-in-Galilee is the first of the .... by which Jesus revealed his glory and led his disciples to believe in him.'

(John chapter 2, verse 11)

2 When do we think John's Gospel was written: AD 70–80, AD 90–100, or AD 120–150?
3 Why is John's Gospel called a 'spiritual' Gospel?
4 John quotes several 'I am' sayings by Jesus. Give *three* examples.
5 'The good shepherd lays down his life for the sheep.' Who are 'the sheep'?
6 John describes seven miracles or signs. Write about *three* of them.
7 Explain how the Eucharist is for John a sign, mentioning especially words and actions of Jesus which John describes in his Gospel.
8 Make a plan of the way John's Gospel proceeds from beginning to end.

5 The Synoptic Problem

What is the Synoptic Problem?

1 Griesbach's Synopsis

Over two hundred years ago a German scholar named Johann Jacob Griesbach printed the three first Gospels side by side in parallel columns. He called his book a Synopsis.

A synopsis is something you can see 'at one glance'. Griesbach wanted to show, 'at one glance', how the first three Gospels, Matthew, Mark and Luke, related to each other. Soon these three Gospels became known as The Synoptic Gospels.

2 Questions to ask

How these three Gospels do relate to each other is the difficult 'Synoptic Problem'. Everyone can see that there is some relationship. They are like three brothers. Maybe there is twenty years difference between two of them. Perhaps two are twins, but not identical twins. One might be bald, another might have grey hair, the third red hair. But all three have their mother's nose. All three smile in the same way. All three stand in the same way. But, since we do not have access to their birth certificates, how are we to guess which is the oldest, which the youngest.

And other questions might arise. Suppose we know their mother married a second time. Have the three brothers the same father?

Such questions occur with Matthew, Mark and Luke. Since we can no longer ask the authors questions, we have to work like detectives on what they wrote. Our questions are:

1 Which was the first Synoptic Gospel to be written?
2 Did the other two copy from it?
3 Have the second two Gospels any other sources in common?
4 Are there any other sources on which the Synoptic Gospels are based?

Which Gospel was written first?

St Augustine

For many many years Christians believed that Matthew's Gospel was written first. That is why it comes first in our present Bibles. St Augustine, writing in the fourth century AD, says Matthew wrote first and Mark wrote a shorter edition of Matthew's Gospel.

Now Mark is certainly shorter than Matthew. And there is hardly anything in Mark's Gospel that we cannot also find in Matthew. These two facts seem to suggest that St Augustine was right, and Matthew's Gospel was the first.

Today's scholar

But most people today do not believe this. In looking at the Synoptic Problem, scholars nearly all argue that Mark wrote the first Gospel and that Matthew and Luke copied from him.

Here are some of their reasons:

1 Matthew is more concise than Mark

Whenever Matthew and Mark tell the same story, Mark's is the longest version, Matthew's the shortest. This suggests that if one is copying from the other, it is Matthew, not Mark. Contrary to St Augustine's statement, Matthew is cutting down Mark, not the other way round.

You can see this happening in the following example:

Matthew chapter 13, verses 54 and 55	Mark chapter 6, verses 1 and 2
'And coming into his own country he taught them in their synagogue,	'He went away from there and came to his own country; and his disciples followed him. And on the sabbath he began to teach in the synagogue,

so that they were astonished,

and said, "Where did this man get his wisdom and these mighty works?"'

and many who heard him were astonished, saying, "Where did this man get all this? What is the wisdom given to him? What mighty works are done by his hands!"'

2 Nearly every part of Mark appears in Matthew and Luke

There are slight changes in these parts but they are recognisably the same.

Mark has in fact 661 verses. Of these, 606 appear in Matthew and 320 appear in Luke. (Only 31 of Mark's verses appear in neither of the other two Synoptic Gospels.)

3 Mark is the least concise

Where Matthew, Mark and Luke use the same story, Mark always gives the longest version. You can see this, for example, if you compare how all three Gospels recount that Jesus healed a leper:

- Matthew chapter 8, verses 1 to 4
- Mark chapter 1, verses 40 to 45
- Luke chapter 5, verses 12 to 16

4 Mark decided the order of events and stories

Sometimes of course Matthew or Luke decided to change Mark's order. But they never both contradict Mark. If Luke changes the order of Mark, Matthew does not. If Matthew changes the order of Mark, Luke does not. This clue takes a little puzzling over, but it indicates that Mark is the one from whom the others are copying.

5 Matthew and Luke make changes

Matthew and Luke change things that might embarrass the Christian communities they are living in and who would read their Gospels. You can see this in the account of the healing of the leper, which we mention above. Mark says that Jesus was angry when the leper came to him. Matthew and Luke do not like repeating that Jesus was angry. They probably did not believe he could have been angry with a leper. So they say, instead, that he was 'moved with compassion'. You can understand such a change. It is scarcely possible to believe that Mark, copying one of the others, would have changed the description the other way.

One of the very few passages in Mark not found anywhere else, either in Matthew or Luke, is chapter 3, verses 20 and 21. 'Then Jesus went home; and the crowd came together again, so that he could not even eat. And when his family heard it, they went out to seize him, for people were saying, "He is beside himself".'

To see this concern for Jesus's good name, compare:

- Mark chapter 3, verses 1 to 6, with
- Matthew chapter 12, verses 9 to 14 and
- Luke chapter 6, verses 6 to 11.

It is difficult to imagine Mark altering Luke's version or Matthew's version. Again, we deduce that Mark wrote first; the others copied — and changed — what he had written.

6 More changes by Matthew and Luke

Just as Matthew and Luke worry about the reputation of Jesus and alter stories if they think these reflect badly on Jesus's good name, so they alter stories which suggest criticism of Jesus's disciples.

We have already seen that there is reason to believe part of Mark's Gospel comes from Peter's memories. Peter would no longer have minded appearing in a bad light. He knew that Jesus had forgiven him. Matthew and Luke were more sensitive, so they altered Mark.

You can see this happening in the following example, part of Jesus's parable of the sower:

Matthew chapter 13, verse 18	Mark chapter 4, verse 13	Luke chapter 8, verse 11
'Hear then the parable of the sower.'	'And he said to them, "Do you not understand this parable? How then will you understand all the parables?"'	'Now the parable is this: the seed is the word of God.'

Luke and Matthew have here decidedly toned down Jesus's criticism of his disciples, which Mark was perfectly willing to publicise. You can find another example of this by comparing:

- Mark chapter 10, verse 35, 'And James and John, the sons of Zebedee, came forward to Jesus and said to him, "Teacher, we want you to do for us whatever we ask of you",' with the corresponding passage in:
- Matthew chapter 20, verse 20, 'Then the mother of the sons of Zebedee came up to Jesus with her sons, and kneeling before him she asked him for something.'

Matthew has not only taken out the apparent selfishness of the two disciples. He also puts any blame there might be on to their mother!

For the six reasons given above, today scholars are virtually certain that the resemblances between the first three Gospels arise from the fact that Matthew and Luke both had before them Mark's Gospel. They altered it wherever they felt it necessary. But substantially they both based themselves on Mark.

Here then is a scheme showing the preliminary relationship between the three Synoptic Gospels:

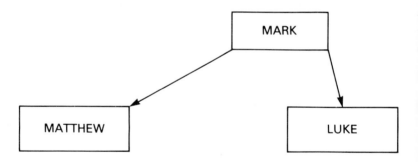

Information found only in Matthew

Both Matthew and Luke also include information about the life and teaching of Jesus found nowhere else in the New Testament.

1 References to the Old Testament

Matthew, as we have seen is especially concerned to show

Below: Christ's Entry into Jerusalem from a fifteenth century Italian Bible

Jesus as following prophecies set out in the Old Testament. For example, in the Jewish Bible (Zechariah chapter 9, verse 9) a poet wrote:

'Rejoice greatly, O daughter of Zion!
Shout aloud, O daughter of Jerusalem!
Lo, your king comes to you;
triumphant and victorious is he,
humble and riding on an ass,
on a colt, the foal of an ass.'

Journey to Jerusalem

Matthew knew that Jesus rode into Jerusalem on a donkey. But did not Zechariah suggest that the true king of the Jews rode on *two* animals? Matthew (in chapter 21) tells us that this is precisely what Jesus did. And we can find other examples of special material in Matthew closely linking what Jesus did with texts of the Old Testament.

2 The law

Matthew is also particularly concerned with how Jesus regarded the Jewish law. Part of his Sermon on the Mount, not found in any other Gospel, deals with this (chapter 5, verses 17 to 20). Most of chapter 23 follows the same theme and is once again peculiar to Matthew alone.

A good number of Matthew's parables deal with this theme too. Some have extremely powerful, trenchant meanings. They include:

the parable of the weeds among the wheat (chapter 13, verses 24 to 30 and 36 to 43);
the parable of the dragnet (chapter 13, verses 47 to 50);
the parable of the unmerciful servant (chapter 18, verses 23 to 35);
the parable of the wise and foolish young women (chapter 25, verses 1 to 13);
the parable of the Last Judgment — the sheep and the goats (chapter 25, verses 31 to 46).

3 Material special to 'M'

Finally Matthew includes a few stories that obviously fascinated the circles for whom he wrote and from whom he derived his material. He tells us, for instance, about the end of Judas, who betrayed Jesus. (He hanged himself, says Matthew, chapter 27. The Acts of the Apostles, chapter 1, verse 18, says Judas died differently: he fell in a field and 'he burst open in the middle, and all his bowels gushed out'.)

No one knows where this material all came from before Matthew included it in his Gospel. But scholars, reasonably enough, call it 'M', i.e. the special material of Matthew.

Information found only in Luke

Luke similarly has his own special material. He alone tells us about Jesus as a young man (Luke chapter 2, verses 41 to 52).

1 Miracles

Luke too has in his Gospels accounts of miracles not found in any other Gospel; for example:

the raising from death of a widow's son (chapter 7, verses 11 to 17);
the healing of a man with dropsy (chapter 14, verses 1 to 6).

the healing of ten lepers (chapter 17, verses 11 to 19);

2 Parables

Even more influential than these in Christian history have been a series of astonishingly powerful parables found only in Luke's Gospel. These are:

the parable of the good Samaritan (chapter 10, verses 30 to 37);
the parable of the rich fool (chapter 12, verses 13 to 21);
the parable of the prodigal son (chapter 15, verses 11 to 32);
the parable of the unjust steward (chapter 16, verses 1 to 8);
the parable of the rich man and Lazarus (chapter 16, verses 19 to 31);
the parable of the Pharisee and the publican (chapter 18, verses 9 to 14).

**The woman
sinner**

Luke also includes one of his most moving stories in the one (which he takes from Mark) about how Jesus ate at the house of a Pharisee named Simon. The story concerns a sinner, a woman, who washes Jesus's feet with her tears, wipes them with her hair, and anoints him with precious ointment. Simon thinks, 'If this man were a prophet, he would have known who and what sort of woman this is who is touching him, for she is a sinner.' Jesus rebukes Simon, saying, 'Her sins, which are many, are forgiven, for she loved much.' (chapter 7, verses 36 to 50)

3 Material special to 'L'

As with Matthew, Luke's special material tells us much about his particular interests:

his concern for the underprivileged, such as widows;
his attitude to the poor and the rich;
his love for outsiders, such as Samaritans.

As with Matthew, we do not know how this material reached Luke; but scholars have found it reasonable to call it 'L', i.e. the special material found only in Luke.

Other sources for Matthew and Luke

If we cut out of Matthew and Luke everything that seems to have come from Mark's Gospel, we still find that they have a lot in common. Look for example at:

Matthew chapter 7, verses 7 to 10	Luke chapter 11, verses 9 to 12
'Ask, and it will be given you; seek, and you will find; knock, and it will be opened to you. For every one who asks receives, and he who seeks finds, and to him who knocks it will be opened. Or what man of you, if his son asks him for a fish, will give him a serpent?'	'And I tell you, Ask and it will be given you; seek, and you will find, knock, and it will be opened to you. For every one who asks receives, and he who seeks, finds, and to him who knocks it will be opened. What father among you, if his son asks for a fish, will instead of a fish given him a serpent; or if he asks for an egg, will give him a scorpion?'

1 'Q' — one common source?

Although there are a good many such passages, clearly somehow related to each other, they don't always appear in the same order in Matthew and Luke. Sometimes Matthew and Luke disagree about when and where Jesus spoke sayings they have in common. This is especially true, for instance, of Matthew's Sermon on the Mount (chapter 5, particularly verses 1 to 12) and Luke's Sermon on the Plain (chapter 6, verses 17 to 23), which both contain the 'Beatitudes'.

Sermon on the Mount

Sermon on the Plain

Yet, in spite of these differences, it seems hard to believe that there was not some common source for those parts of Jesus's life and teaching that both Matthew and Luke tell us about. However, no one has ever found such a document.

Perhaps one day someone will. For the present, people call this source — which no one has seen — 'Q'. ('Q' is the first letter of the German word *Quelle*, which means 'source'.)

Those who don't believe in 'Q' sometimes object that either Luke or Matthew could have copied from the other. But this isn't likely since (as we have already seen), those sections they have in common appear at widely different parts of their narratives. They felt free to insert segments from 'Q' into their Gospels according to their own differing interests and in their own order.

2 'Q' — several sources?

Even so, it might easily be that, instead of one document, 'Q' represents several sources. Luke at the beginning of his Gospel writes of 'many' persons who had written narratives of what had happened as a result of the coming of Jesus. He claimed to have written about events and teaching 'delivered to us by those who from the beginning were eyewitnesses' of what had happened. Perhaps several documents made up what we now see as the 'Q' material of Matthew and Luke.

And in addition, we do not need to believe that what we have isolated reached Matthew and Luke as documents. In those days many believers committed the words of Jesus to memory and handed them on in this form to their fellow-Christians. We call this 'oral tradition'. Matthew and Luke might easily have derived much, if not all, of their 'Q' material from oral tradition.

But with all these reservations, common material does exist in these two Gospels; and we therefore need to add to our plan showing the relationship between the three Synoptic Gospels a source called 'Q':

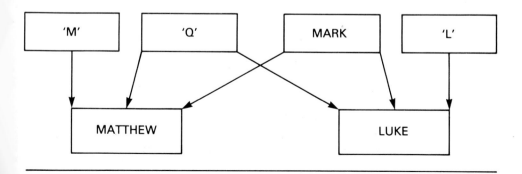

1 What is a synopsis and which Gospels are the Synoptic Gospels?
2 Give three reasons why many people believe that Mark wrote the first Gospel and Matthew and Luke copied from him.
3 Matthew and Luke try to protect the reputation of Jesus's disciples. Give two examples of this.
4 The Sermon on the Mount is found only in Matthew's Gospel, Mark's Gospel, Luke's Gospel or John's Gospel?
5 State which Gospels the following parables come from: the good Samaritan; the healing of the man with dropsy; the Pharisee and the publican.
6 'As Jesus grew up he advanced in wisdom and in favour with God and men.' In which Gospel is this information found?
7 What do we mean by 'Q', 'L' and 'M'?
8 Who wrote down in his Gospel the Sermon on the Plain?
9 Find in different Gospels four accounts of Jesus's life and teaching which are identical, word for word.
10 From your reading of Luke's Gospel quote two stories that show his interest in *outsiders* and *non-Jews*.

6 Other Ways of Looking at the Gospels

Form Criticism

1 The oral tradition

Obviously, from our study of the Synoptic Problem, we must conclude that a Gospel is something far more complex than one man's personal memories of the life and teaching of Jesus. Our Gospels are documents built out of complex sources by Christians who passionately wished to present their own, committed view of Jesus.

What is more, if we take seriously the notion of oral tradition already mentioned, the Gospels reflect the needs of various communities in the early church. The earliest Christians expected Jesus soon to return after his ascent into heaven. They felt no need to write down the events of his life or the elements of his teaching. In any case, books were expensive, and the Jews had for centuries cultivated the art of memorising important episodes in their history and reciting them among their communities.

You can read evidence that the early Christians did this. In the opening words of his Gospel Luke says he has drawn on
Eyewitnesses   the words of eyewitnesses of what had happened. Again, when St Paul tells of the Last Supper and the beginning of the Christian Eucharist, he says that he 'passed on' to others the account he himself 'had been told'. Similarly he says elsewhere he is passing on what he has received from others about Jesus's death. The Gospels were formed by
Word of mouth   word of mouth.

So, many of the events and stories we read of in the Gospels had been handed on for dozens of years in the church before being written down. These short tales, committed to memory, would be repeated most of all when

Christians were talking about Jesus in synagogues and when they met for the Eucharist. And the preacher who repeated these stories would obviously try to show how they applied to the present lives of those who were listening to him.

Did this affect the stories themselves? A group of scholars, **Form Critics** who call themselves Form Critics, think it did.

2 Conflict stories

For instance, slowly the Jewish authorities came to think the Christians were unwelcome in the Temple and the synagogues. In such situations the Christians would ask themselves whether Jesus had met any such opposition. They began to collect what the Form Critics call 'conflict stories'. In Mark's Gospel, chapter 2 and chapter 3, verses 1 to 6, you can read no fewer than five of these, one after the other:

1 Jesus heals a paralysed man — and some Jewish leaders object because Jesus claims to forgive his sins.
2 Jesus calls Levi as a disciple — and some Jewish leaders object that Levi and other friends of Jesus are tax collectors.
3 Jesus argues with the Pharisees, because he and his do not fast.
4 Jesus defends his disciples for eating grain they have harvested on the Sabbath (when the Jewish law said a Jew must not work on the Sabbath).
5 Again on the Sabbath day Jesus heals a man with a withered hand. The Pharisees object, and Jesus asks, 'Is it lawful on the Sabbath to do good or to do harm, to save life or to kill?'

These stories are designed:

1 to help explain how Jewish leaders at that time turned against Jesus (according to Mark chapter 3, verse 6, 'The Pharisees went out, and immediately held counsel with the Herodians against him, how they might destroy him');
2 to demonstrate that Jesus was in no way at fault during these conflicts;

3 to show that only the leaders of the Jews opposed Jesus, whereas people in general flocked to him.

The needs of the early church explain why these particular stories about Jesus, rather than the many others that must have existed, were preserved and eventually written down in our four Gospels

3 Modified stories and different explanations

But some Form Critics go further. They say that some stories have been modified by the early church; or else the story has been preserved accurately enough, but later explanations change.

Parable of the sower

Explanations of Jesus's parables certainly differ in the Gospels. Compare the explanations of the parable of the sower, in:

- Matthew chapter 13, verses 19 to 23;
- Mark chapter 4, verses 14 to 20;
- Luke chapter 8, verses 11 to 15.

May we reasonably conclude that the parable is an accurate memory of the words of Jesus, but that the explanations were added later?

4 Invented stories

Other Form Critics have claimed that some stories about Jesus were even invented by the early church. They call

Sacred legends

these 'sacred legends' and would include among them:

the stories of the birth of Jesus in Matthew and Luke;
Jesus walking on water, in Matthew chapter 14, Mark chapter 6 and John chapter 6;
Jesus stilling a storm, in Matthew chapter 8, Mark chapter 4 and Luke chapter 8.

We need not go so far as those Form Critics who believe Gospel stories to have been seriously modified or even invented to accept that many events and stories preserved for us in the Gospels are there because they were used to serve the church of that time. They had been preserved by Christian communities who needed to apply the life and teaching of Jesus to their own problems and difficulties.

Redaction Criticism

1 A necklace

The four Gospels remind us of the making of a necklace.

The jeweller has a box of beads, of precious stones, of brightly coloured treasures. Some of them may already have been strung together. But it is up to him to decide in the end which to use. The jeweller creates the pattern of the necklace out of lots of smaller pieces, imposing on them his own vision.

Those who created the Gospels behaved exactly like this. The Redaction Critics point out that the way the Gospels are put together reveals to us the mind of their creator — just as the pattern of the necklace expresses the vision of the jeweller who created it. The Gospel-writer selects his material according to his own special cares and concerns.

Matthew and the church

So, a Redaction Critic argues, we can see that Matthew is fascinated by the church: he sets out rules for the church; he works out who is head of the church; he closely aligns the kingdom of God with the church.

Mark and the Messianic secret

By contrast we can see that Mark worries about the Messianic secret of Jesus, and collects material to defend this idea.

Luke and outsiders

Luke selects stories that fit in with his fascination for outsiders and non-Jews, cutting out anything that might puzzle his non-Jewish readers.

John and the spiritual reality

John's standpoint leads him to emphasise the spiritual reality behind concrete events and things, arranging his Gospel to proclaim this.

The above four points are a very crude summary of some of the insights the Redaction Critics can bring to the study of the four Gospels.

Redaction comes from the German word for an editor. If you compare how the different Gospel-writers deal with the same story you can often see the 'editor' that each one was, at work. You can often look into his mind as he is working.

2 An example: the withered fig tree

Mark's version of the story tells how Jesus goes to Jerusalem, enters the Temple and then returns to Bethany:

Mark's version

'On the following day, when they came from Bethany, he was hungry. And seeing in the distance a fig tree in leaf, he went to see if he could find anything on it. When he came to it he found nothing but leaves, for it was not the season for figs. And he said to it, "May no one ever eat fruit from you again." And his disciples heard it.' Then Jesus goes again to Jerusalem and throws out of the Temple those who are abusing it. He and his disciples again leave Jerusalem. 'As they passed by in the morning they saw the fig tree withered away to its roots. And Peter remembered and said to him, "Master, look! The fig tree which you cursed has withered." And Jesus answered them, "Have faith in God . . .".'

(Mark chapter 11, verses 12 to 14, 20 to 22)

Now this is an extremely strange story — on the face of it. First, the fig tree apparently ought not to have borne fruit just then. But this might be misleading. Sometimes, we know, figs in that part of the world grew out of season on fig trees. Secondly, was there a miracle or not? Was it simply an accident that the fig tree was found withered shortly after Jesus cursed it? We are not told by Mark.

But none of this counts for Mark. He sees the fig tree as symbolising two things:

faith can work wonders;
faithless Jerusalem will be rejected, the Temple destroyed just as the fig tree withered.

Matthew changes the story. His version, in chapter 21, is much shorter:

Matthew's version

'In the morning, as he was returning to the city, he was hungry. And seeing a fig tree by the wayside he went to it and found nothing on it but leaves only. And he said to it, "May no fruit ever come from you again!" And the fig tree withered at once. When the disciples saw it, they marvelled, saying, "How did the fig tree wither at once?" And Jesus answered them, "Truly, I say to you, if you have faith and never doubt, you will not only do what has been done to the fig tree . . .".'

(Matthew chapter 21, verses 18 to 21)

The difference is striking:

the fig tree withers instantly.

The point the story makes are the same as in Mark, but Matthew has made it far more miraculous. And Matthew often does this in his Gospel. He heightens the miraculous.

Luke's parallel   Luke's parallel to this miracle brings a further surprise. Many modern Christians have held this to be a somewhat unreasonable miracle. So, apparently, did Luke. His Gospel contains no such miracle. Instead he substitutes a parable:

'A man had a fig tree planted in his vineyard; and he came seeking fruit on it and found none. And he said to the vinedresser, "Lo, these three years have I come seeking fruit on this tree, and I find none. Cut it down. Why should it use up the ground?" And the vinedresser answered him, "Leave it alone, sir, for this year too, till I dig about it and put on manure. And if it bears fruit next year, well and good; but if not, you can cut it down".'

(Luke chapter 13, verses 6 to 9)

Again the point of the parable is the same as the lessons drawn in Mark and Matthew from the withered fig tree. Luke, like the other two Gospel-writers, knows that a question-mark hangs over the future of Jerusalem. But here he shows:

a different attitude to such strange miracles as the cursing of a fig tree;
much greater 'humanity', far more gentleness than his two fellow writers.

Simply by analysing how the Gospel-writers *edit* their material we can see, as this single example demonstrates, deep aspects of their subtle and sometimes differing faiths.

It also forces us to ask what *we* really believe about these stories. What is the meaning of the fruitless fig tree today? Do we believe that a nation, city or person that refuses to follow the laws of God eventually withers away?

An equally important question is the meaning of Jesus's reply to the statement that the fig tree had withered. What was he telling his disciples?

The essence of a Gospel

1 Not simply a work of history

What, then, is a Gospel? Obviously, from what we have seen, the four Gospel-writers were not interested simply in giving the *facts* of Jesus's life.

They passionately wanted to persuade their readers that their own *attitude* to these facts was correct and ought to be shared. They wanted to make others believe what they believed. They are not writing biographies of Jesus. They are preaching that Jesus is the Christ.

Good news

So we have to use their word: 'Gospel'. Gospel means 'good news'. We have the good news:

as Matthew saw it;
as Mark saw it;
as Luke saw it;
as John saw it.

2 Spiritual sight

They expect the good news to dawn on their readers too.

Mark expresses this marvellously. In chapter 8, verses 22 to 26, he tells how Jesus healed a blind man. Slowly the man came to see. At first, he said, he saw people, 'but they look like trees walking'. Finally he sees everything clearly. Jesus tells him to tell no one of this (the Messianic secret at work).

Messianic secret

Shortly afterwards — at last — Peter realises who Jesus is. So Mark's story of a man gradually given physical sight shows us the pattern of how Peter (and we too) arrive at spiritual sight. And as with the blind man, so with Peter, Jesus says no one must be told what has happened.

Mark has put these stories together because they fit in with his own view of the Christian faith. The Gospels give us the deep, subtle faith of four early Christian geniuses. As we have seen, they sometimes differ from each other. But all of them (not just Mark) write because they themselves believe in the good news about Jesus and they want others to believe in it.

Spiritual sight

1 Fill in the words missing from the following passage:

When Jesus was at table in his house, many bad characters — tax-gatherers and others — were seated with him and his disciples; for there were many who followed him. Some doctors of the law who were .... noticed him eating in this bad company, and said to his ...., 'He eats with tax-gatherers and sinners!' Jesus overheard and said to them, 'It is not the healthy that need a doctor, but the sick; I did not come to invite virtuous people, but sinners.'

Once, when John's disciples and the .... were keeping a fast, some people came to him and said, 'Why is it that John's disciples and the disciples of the .... are fasting, but yours are not?' Jesus said to them, 'Can you expect the bridegroom's friends to fast while the bridegroom is with them? As long as they have the bridegroom with them, there can be no fasting. But the time will come when the bridegroom will be taken away from them, and on that day they will fast.

(Mark chapter 2, verses 19 to 20)

2 Fill in the words missing from the following passage:

One .... he was going through the cornfields; and his disciples as they went, began to pluck ears of corn. The .... said to him, 'Look, why are they doing what is forbidden on the ....?' He answered, 'Have you never read what David did when he and his men were hungry had nothing to eat? He went into the House of God, in the time of Abiathar the High Priest, and ate the consecrated loaves, though no one but a priest is allowed to eat them, and even gave them to his men.'

(Mark chapter 2, verses 23 to 26)

Look up Jesus's conclusion in the verses that follow.

3 The Gospel stories were formed by 'oral tradition'. What does this statement mean?
4 List three 'conflict stories' from the Gospels.
5 Which of the four Gospel-writers was fascinated by the church?
6 Matthew, Mark and Luke all include in their Gospels a story about a fig tree — though they treat this story in different ways, showing their different interests. Illustrate this.

7 The Background to the Gospels

The Jerusalem Temple

The first Jerusalem Temple had long since been destroyed and several times rebuilt. About forty years before the birth of Jesus King Herod the Great ordered the rebuilding of a magnificent new Temple. By 9 BC most of it was complete — though it was not completely finished until AD 64, four years before the Romans destroyed it.

Set on a great esplanade measuring almost 500 by 300 metres, built of great stone, embellished with precious marbles and gold, the Temple was the centre of the worship of the orthodox Jew. One of Jesus's disciples said to him, 'Look, teacher, what wonderful stones and what wonderful buildings!' as he and the rest of Jesus's company left the Temple one day. Jesus replied, 'Do you see these great buildings? There will not be left here one stone upon another, that will not be thrown down.' (Mark chapter 13, verses 1 and 2)

Non-Jews
By now non-Jews were allowed into the outer parts of the Temple. Two great inscriptions told these non-Jews that they went further into the Temple at the risk of their lives.

The famous 'Beautiful Gate' led into a courtyard reserved for Jewish women, beyond which was found the court of Israel, where men worshipped, and — even further towards the most sacred spot of the whole Temple — the court of the priests. This contained the great altar, 25 metres long and seven and a half metres high. On this altar, twice a day was sacrificed a lamb. And throughout the day this altar was the scene of countless private sacrifices. Sacrificial animals were sold in the court of the non-Jews, and here too money was exchanged for Temple offerings. (The technical term for these non-Jews is 'Gentiles'.)

Beyond the great altar was the Holy of Holies. This most

A model of the
Jerusalem
Temple at the
time of Herod

sacred spot had once contained the ancient 'Ark' of the Jews,
but this had long since disappeared. The Holy of Holies in
Jesus's time was empty. It was separated from the rest of the
Temple by a huge veil; and once a year the high priest, on
behalf of the whole people, passed beyond this veil into the
Holy of Holies.

When Jesus died on the cross, Matthew tells us, the veil of
the Temple was torn in two, as if there was now no barrier
between God and man.

Plan of Herod's Temple in Jerusalem

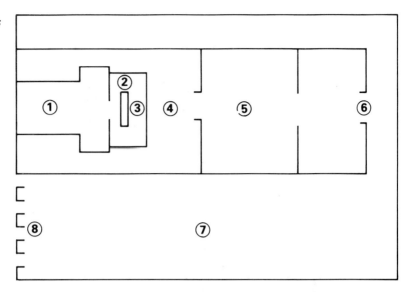

1 Holy of Holies
2 Altar
3 Court of the priests
4 Court of Jewish men

5 Court of Jewish women
6 Beautiful Gate
7 Court of non-Jews (the Gentiles)
8 Porticos

Try to describe and draw from memory the Jerusalem Temple.

All sorts of people

1 The high priest

The high priest was the most important of all the Jerusalem clergy. He alone had the right, once a year, to enter the Holy of Holies. Though the high priest had the leading role among the Jewish people, his position was less secure after the Roman rulers of Jerusalem insisted on the right to re-appoint high priests in succession, instead of following the old custom where these men held the office for life. From that change onwards the high priests had to try to please their Roman rulers.

A nineteenth
century
engraving of a
high priest

2 The Sadducees

From this group of aristocratic priests was almost always
drawn the high priest. Sadducees were devoted to the first
five books of the Old Testament and did not like most of what
they read elsewhere. (As a result, for instance, they did not
believe in the resurrection, and in Mark, chapter 12, verses
18 to 27, we find them arguing with Jesus about this.) These
men provided the Temple priests. To preserve their power,
they tended to collaborate with the occupying Roman

authority. Ironically, they did not survive as a group the destruction of the Temple by the Romans in AD 70.

3 The Pharisees

Pharisees, though in the New Testament always seeming at odds with Jesus, were in fact Jews of high moral integrity. They did not care much for politics, separating themselves from what they regarded as sinful mixing with the world (the word 'Pharisee' means 'separated one'). Longing to keep the law of God, they worked out more and more elaborate rules for doing so. (One Pharisee, criticised in a parable of Jesus, even so fasted twice a week and gave away a tenth of all his money — see Luke chapter 18, verses 9 to 14.)

Some of these Pharisees were extremely interested in what Jesus had to say. (Luke tells us of one who especially asked to eat with him, and of others who came to warn him to escape because Herod wanted to kill him.) Although they numbered probably fewer than six thousand in all, their faith was strong enough to survive the destruction wrought by the Romans in AD 70 — and their example undoubtedly helped the rest of the Jewish people to survive this disaster.

For these reasons it is important to ask ourselves why Jesus is shown as quarrelling so much with the Pharisees.

First, read the whole parable in Luke chapter 18, verses 9 to 14. Is there a complete difference here between Jesus's notion of being saved and that of the Pharisees?

Secondly, are some angry remarks made by Jesus about the Pharisees, for example in Luke chapter 11, verses 42 etc.), overemphasised by the Gospel-writers because of later quarrels between Christians and the Jewish leaders? Pharisees quarrelled with Jesus over:

1 **the Sabbath**   This was the seventh day of the week, when all work was forbidden — though the sacrifices prescribed in the Old Testament had been doubled on this day.

'One Sabbath Jesus walked through the grainfields. His disciples began to pluck the heads of grain. The Pharisees said, "What they are doing is not lawful on the Sabbath." Jesus, pointing out that even King David broke rules when he thought it right, said, "The Sabbath was made for man; not man for the Sabbath; and the son of man is lord even of the Sabbath".'

(Mark chapter 2, verses 23 to 28)

2 **his friendship with tax collectors and sinners**

3 **fasting**

(Mark chapter 2, verses 15 to 19)

4 **ritual washing**
(Matthew chapter 15, verses 1 and 2; Mark chapter 7, verses
1 to 4)

Pharisees also quarrelled with Jesus because:

5 some of them were **hypocrites**.
(Luke chapter 11, verses 37 to 44, and chapter 12, verse 1)

4 The scribes

These are often linked with the Pharisees in our Gospels,
and in fact many were Pharisees. Not all of them, though.
They gathered round themselves disciples, as Jesus did, and
taught them the details of the Jewish law. So they were
called 'Doctors of the Law', and very highly esteemed. You
had to study till you were nearly forty years old to become a
scribe. Scribes were often given the honourable title 'rabbi'.

Doctors of the Law

5 Country priests

There were seven thousand or so of these, many of them
poor enough to have to work in ordinary tasks. But they had
the honour of serving in the Temple in rotation — divided up
into twenty-four groups for this purpose.

6 The Levites

The Levites obeyed and served the priests in the worship of
the Temple, bringing them wood and water and also singing
and playing musical instruments. There were a lot of them —
nearly ten thousand. They, like the country priests, were
divided into twenty-four sections, to serve in the Temple.

7 The Gentiles

Gentiles are, quite simply, all non-Jews. Some of these had
decided to become Jews. They were called proselytes.
Proselytes were circumcised. They were baptised. They
accepted all the Jewish laws.

Proselytes

In the Jerusalem Temple was a special separate courtyard where Gentiles were allowed to gather.

The Gospels stress Jesus's special concern for Gentiles (see for instance the healing of the centurion's servant and the parable of the good Samaritan, Matthew chapter 8, verses 5 to 13; Luke chapter 7 verses 1 to 10; Luke chapter 10, verses 30 to 37) partly no doubt because most Jews had rejected the Gospel message.

8 The Samaritans

The Samaritans had been brought into the country of Samaria by the King of Assyria and had replaced the Israelites who lived there. They had built their own Temple (though the orthodox Jews destroyed it a century or so before the birth of Jesus). The Jews, it was said, had no dealings with the Samaritans. Yet these Samaritans accepted as their Holy Bible the same books as the orthodox Jews.

Jesus did not share the attitude of his fellow-Jews to these people. Luke (chapter 10, verses 30 to 37) records an important parable of Jesus in which a Samaritan is the hero. He was willing to reveal himself as the Messiah to a Samaritan woman (according to John chapter 4, verses 7 to 26). (Read also Luke's story of how Jesus healed ten lepers — chapter 17, verses 11 to 19 — to see how Jesus evokes faith in another Samaritan.)

According to the Acts of the Apostles, the Christian mission first developed amongst the Samaritans.

9 The Romans

Jesus was born, lived and died in the tiny province of the Roman Empire called Palestine. Pompey had conquered the region for the Romans in 63 BC.

Herod the Great

Palestine was ruled during Jesus's time first by Herod the Great, appointed king by the Romans. One Gospel tells us that he tried to have the infant Jesus killed (Matthew chapter 2). Next Herod Antipas, who ruled in Galilee, had John the Baptist killed. Later this same Herod Antipas met Jesus (according to Luke chapter 23, verses 6 to 12) and mocked him.

Herod Antipas

Pontius Pilate

But the Roman chiefly responsible for allowing Jesus to be put to death was Pontius Pilate. He governed Judea from AD 26 onwards. We know that the Jews disliked him for allowing

The Greek
Church at
Cana, Galilee

Roman soldiers to march into Jerusalem bearing their standards. We also know he was a weak man, since he immediately gave way to the outcry over this. Matthew's Gospel says he weakly tried to get out of responsibility for Jesus's death.

Nero

The activities of one Roman emperor — Nero — are not mentioned in the Gospels; but they affected the attitudes of Christians. Nero in AD 64 attempted to avoid blame for a disastrous fire in Rome by blaming the Christians for it. He put many of them to death.

10 Tax collectors

Romans

The Romans, wherever they went, imposed taxes, and those who collected them were especially unpopular. Some of them cheated. Jesus chose one of them as a disciple. His friendship with tax collectors offended many people; and he refused to condemn paying taxes to the Romans, provided this did not conflict with what we owe to God.

11 The Zealots

Destruction of the Temple

Jesus also chose a Zealot as a disciple. Now the Zealots were the exact opposite of the tax collectors. Far from co-operating with the Roman rule, they were determined to rebel against it. In the end a great Zealot rebellion led to the destruction by the Romans of the Jerusalem Temple (AD 70).

Institutions

1 The Council of the Jews

This council had a special name — the *Sanhedrin*. It helped to condemn Jesus to death. Head of the Sanhedrin was the high priest. Its other seventy members were either scribes or Pharisees.

The Council met in the Jerusalem Temple twice a week. It **religious** had religious duties:
duties

fixing the religious events of the year;
deciding on true teachings.

worldly duties It had also worldly duties:

running a police force;
it could turn itself into a court of law.

Although the Council had the power to condemn Jesus to death, it was not allowed by the Romans to carry out such a sentence.

Throughout Palestine were little councils. Matthew tells us that Jesus told his disciples to expect to fall foul of them: 'People will deliver you up to councils and flog you in their synagogues.' (Matthew chapter 10, verse 17)

2 The synagogues

Just as there were many little councils, matching the one great Council of Jerusalem, so there were many synagogues — the place where each little village worshipped each Saturday. The men and women would sit separately, listening to men who read from the Jewish Bible and told them what it meant. Here too was the local school.

Luke tells us that Jesus went to the synagogue of Nazareth regularly every Saturday. He himself used to read from the Old Testament and say what he thought it meant. Sometimes he pleased the people by this (read Luke chapter 4, verses 16 to 22). At other times he offended them (read Mark chapter 6, verses 1 to 3).

Eventually the Christians were no longer welcome to worship or teach in synagogues. They explained the Old Testament in a way that offended most Jews.

A model of
Jerusalem at
the time of
Herod

QUESTIONS

1 Draw a plan of Herod's Temple in Jerusalem. Show where
  were the Holy of Holies, the Beautiful Gate and the Altar.
2 Matthew tells us that when Jesus died on the cross the
  .... of the Temple was ....
3 Say what you know about the Sadducees.
4 The .... was the most important of all the
  Jerusalem clergy. Once a year he entered the

  ....
5 Name three topics over which Jesus and the Pharisees
  disagreed.

6 Describe briefly the scribes, the Levites, Zealots and proselytes.

8 One of Jesus's disciples was a tax collector. Why did the friendship between Jesus and tax collectors offend so many people?

9 The Council of the Jews at Jerusalem was called the .... What were its duties?

10 Imagine you were attending a synagogue when Jesus was there. Describe what happened.

11 Choose a word (or words) from modern everyday usage which you think might mean something similar to the idea of 'Messiah'. Explain why you have chosen this word and how it helps to illustrate the way in which Jesus is regarded by Christians today.

12 If a Pharisee and a Sadducee had a conversation, what would they talk about that would reveal their differences in belief?

13 What does Luke's Gospel tell us about the people who came to see Jesus at his birth?

14 Who came to worship the child Jesus, according to Matthew's Gospel?

15 Fill in the missing words in the following parable:

'A man was on his way from Jerusalem down to Jericho when he fell in with robbers, who stripped him, beat him, and went off leaving him half dead. It so happened that a .... was going down by the same road; but when he saw him, he went past on the other side. So too a .... came to the place, and when he saw him went past on the other side. But a .... who was making the journey came upon him, and when he saw him was moved to pity. He went up and bandaged his wounds, bathing them with oil and wine. Then he lifted him on to his own beast, brought him to an inn, and looked after him there. Next day he produced two silver pieces and gave them to the inn-keeper, and said, "Look after him; and if you spend any more, I will repay you on my way back."'

(Luke chapter 10, verses 30 to 36)

What do you think is the message of this parable for us today?

16 What led to the destruction of the Jerusalem Temple in the year AD 70?

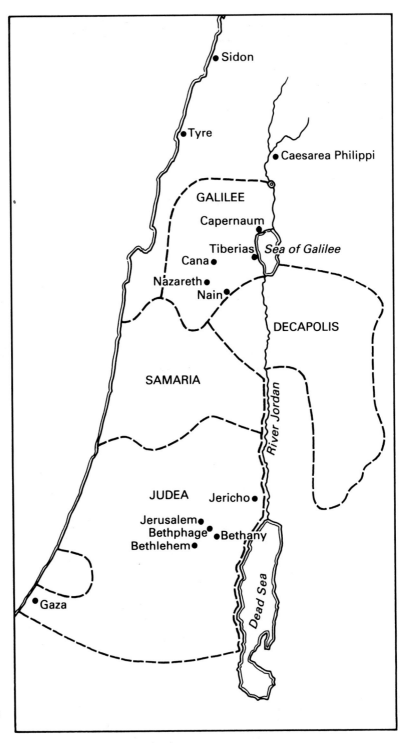

Palestine at the time of Jesus

8 The Birth of Jesus

The sources

1 Matthew's Gospel

Matthew begins with Jesus's family tree, traced back to
Abraham. Then he tells us that Jesus's mother, Mary, was
'betrothed' to a man named Joseph. She was found to be
pregnant — though the baby was not Joseph's. An angel
from God appeared to Joseph in a dream, saying that the
baby came from the Holy Spirit. The baby, said the angel,
was to be called Jesus.

(Matthew chapter 1)

2 Luke's Gospel

Luke also gives us a family tree for Jesus, tracing his family
back to the first man (according to the Old Testament), that
is Adam. He tells us that the angel Gabriel came to Mary,
who was betrothed to Joseph, to tell her she would bear a
son, to be called Jesus. Mary asked how this should happen,
since she was not yet married. The angel said:

'The Holy Spirit will come upon you,
and the power of the Most High will overshadow you;
therefore the child to be born will be called holy,
the son of God.'

Luke next tells us that because of a census everybody in
Palestine had to go back to where he was born. Although
Joseph and Mary lived in Nazareth, Joseph came from
Bethlehem. He and Mary went there. They could find no

*The
Annunciation*
by Martini di
Simone and
Memmi Lippo

room in an inn, so Jesus was born where animals were
stabled and used a manger as a cradle.
(Luke chapter 1, verses 26 to 35; chapter 1, verses 1 to 7;
chapter 3, verses 23 to 38)

Matthew too tells us Jesus was born in Bethlehem, but he
gives no special reason for this.

Two pregnant women rejoice: story and comments

Elizabeth lived in the city of Judah, which was in the hills. Mary went speedily to see her cousin. When she entered Zechariah's house, Elizabeth's baby leaped inside her — as if to acknowledge Mary's baby.

Elizabeth cried to Mary: 'Blessed are you among women, and blessed is the fruit of your womb.'

Mary said:

My soul magnifies the Lord,
and my spirit rejoices in God my Saviour,
for he has regarded the lowliness of his handmaiden;
for from now on all generations will call me blessed;
for the mighty one has done great things for me,
and his name is holy.
His mercy is on those who fear him from one
generation to the next.
With his strong arm he has scattered the proud in the
imagination of their hearts;
he has put down the mighty from their thrones and lifted
up those of low degree;
He has filled the hungry with good things and he has sent
the rich away empty;
he has helped his servant Israel, remembering his mercy,
as he promised to our forefather, Abraham, and his
children for ever.

Mary stayed with Elizabeth for three months before returning home.

(Luke chapter 1, verses 39 to 56)

Mary's hymm (which is parallelled by a song in the Old Testament) is revolutionary:

Jesus will destroy the pride of vain men and women;
Jesus will cast down the mighty and raise the humble;
Jesus will fill the hungry with food and drive away the rich.

Three special points

1 When was Jesus born?

Matthew says this was when Herod the Great was ruling in Palestine. Herod died in 4 BC, so Jesus must have been born before then. Luke says that the census took place when a man named Quirinus was ruling Syria for the Romans. But the only census held when Quirinus ruled took place two years after Herod had died. Most scholars think Luke has made a mistake here.

As we shall see, when Herod learned of Jesus's birth he tried to have him killed. He ordered every boy under the age of two to be slaughtered. So Jesus was born probably two years or so before Herod's death, say in 6 BC.

These days most of us remember the birth of Jesus on Christmas Day, 25 December. There is nothing in the Bible to suggest this. The early church used to celebrate the birth of Jesus on 6 January. Only four centuries later did Christians take up the idea that he was born on 25 December.

2 Why Bethlehem?

Bethlehem is seventy miles from Nazareth, which was the home of Mary and Joseph. Luke finds it odd that they should go there when Mary was pregnant and about to give birth — so he finds the (false) idea that they were sent there because of a census very attractive.

But both he and Matthew record the fact that Jesus was born in Bethlehem for very important reasons:

City of David's birth

1 The greatest king of the Jews so far, David, had been born there. In both family trees, Matthew's and Luke's, it is made clear that Jesus is descended from David. The two Gospels are saying that Jesus, born in the city of David, is to be the new, and in their view, greatest king of the Jews.
2 The prophet Micah had written of Bethlehem:

'from you shall come forth one who is to be ruler in Israel, whose origin is from of old.'

The Holy Family by Rubens

The Messiah   So everyone expected that the new Messiah would be born in Bethlehem. Although Matthew, Luke and the other two Gospels all know that Jesus's home town was Nazareth, they need to show that the town of his birth was Bethlehem.

3 The Virgin Birth

Both Gospels emphasise that Jesus's birth was *an act of God*. He was born without the help of a human father. The power of the Holy Spirit is stressed.

The Virgin Birth is not much mentioned elsewhere in the New Testament. But it is interesting that the citizens of Nazareth, according to Mark's Gospel (chapter 6, verse 3) call Jesus 'the son of Mary' — not 'the son of Joseph'. Paul the apostle also has a strange phrase which shows he knows something of this Virgin Birth. Jesus, he wrote, came from God, who 'sent forth his son, born of a woman.' (Galatians chapter 4, verse 4)

1 Which Gospel traces Jesus's family tree back to Adam? Which traces it back to Abraham?
2 Put into your own words the conversation between Mary and the angel Gabriel.
3 Give two reasons why the Gospel-writers tell us that Jesus was born in Bethlehem.
4 Write in your own words the song Mary sang at Elizabeth's home. Say in what ways it might inspire people today.
5 Why has Mary's song been described as revolutionary?
6 State when you think Jesus was born. Give reasons for your answer.

Worshipping the child: story and comments

According to Luke   Luke says that when Jesus was born shepherds were in the hills near Bethlehem, watching over their sheep at night. God's angel appeared. They were scared, but the angel told them to rejoice, because that day in Bethlehem a child had been born who was to be 'a Saviour, Christ the Lord'.

The angel said that the shepherds would find the baby wrapped in strips of cloth, lying in a trough where animals' food was usually placed. Then the sky was filled with heavenly beings, who sang:

> 'Glory to God in the highest, and on earth peace among men with whom he is pleased.'

The shepherds rushed to see the infant Jesus and his parents.

(Luke chapter 2, verses 8 to 20)

According to Matthew

Wise men, according to Matthew, came 'from the east to Jerusalem'. They had seen a star in the heavens telling them that the King of the Jews had been born. King Herod was troubled by this news. He found out from the leaders of the Jews that everyone expected the King of the Jews to be born in Bethlehem, and he secretly told this to the wise men, asking them to find the baby and come back to tell him where he too could find him.

The wise men went to Bethlehem. The star they had seen in the east shone down over the place where Mary, Joseph and Jesus were staying. The wise men gave them gifts of gold, frankincense and myrrh. But they were warned in a dream not to tell Herod where Jesus was. Joseph too was warned in a dream that Herod wanted to kill Jesus. He took his family to Egypt. Herod in a rage ordered every child under the age of two in the region of Bethlehem to be killed. Joseph brought his family back to Nazareth only when Herod was dead.

(Matthew chapter 2, verses 1 to 15)

1 Shepherds and angels

Outsiders

Both have great significance in Luke's eyes. Shepherds represent the poor, outsiders — for whom Luke has a special interest. God is showing especial love for the weak ones of this world in giving them this news of the birth of his son. And as an additional reminder of how God reverses the orders of society, his son is born not in the house of his parents, but in humble circumstances, in a borrowed stable.

Saviour Christ

Yet the angel calls this humbly born child a 'Saviour, Christ the Lord'. Saviour is a word not used by the other three Gospel-writers about Jesus. Luke mentions it once more. 'Christ the Lord' is a phrase found nowhere else in the Bible.

'Christ' is the Greek word for Messiah — the chosen one of God.

The angel is joined by a heavenly choir whose song shows that blessings come from God not because men and women deserve them but simply because of God's love for them.

2 Wise men

'Magi', as these men were called, came originally from Iran. They were probably astrologers. The gifts they brought Jesus are all products of southern Arabia. But here the story has probably been influenced by two passages from the Old Testament:

> 'All those from Sheba shall come. They shall bring gold and frankincense, and shall proclaim the praise of the Lord.'
>
> (Isaiah chapter 60, verse 6)
>
> 'May the kings of Sheba and Seba bring gifts!
> May all kings fall down before him, and all nations serve him!'
>
> (Psalm 72, verses 10 and 11)

Matthew is telling us that once and for all these Old Testament hopes are coming true.

Later tradition has given these three wise men names (Caspar, Melchior and Balthasar). In Cologne cathedral you can even see the beautiful shrine in which their bodies are said to lie to this day. All this is speculation. But we are probably right to give special meaning to each of their three gifts:

Three gifts

> gold is a gift for Jesus as King;
> frankincense is used to worship a God;
> myrrh stands for the human side of Jesus, and (since it could be used to spice a dead body) may even at this point be reminding us of his future death.

3 Egypt

The prophet Hosea puts into the mouth of God the words 'Out of Egypt I have called my son'. Matthew (again because he loves to see how Jesus's life fits in with the prophecies of the Old Testament) quotes this when he tells the story of how Joseph managed to escape with his family from King Herod.

The Wise Men and the Star, a nineteenth century German engraving

Yet Herod's behaviour could quite easily be historically true. We know from other sources that he was capable of great savagery.

4 Nazareth

All four Gospels refer to Jesus as a man from Nazareth. He is a 'Nazarene'. There is a difference here between Matthew and Luke:

- Matthew has Jesus born in Bethlehem, presumably because his parents lived there. Only after the exile in Egypt did they move to Nazareth.
- Luke has Jesus's parents originally living in Nazareth — so he finds a special reason why Jesus would have been born in Bethlehem.

1 How did the wise men trick King Herod, and what did Herod do after this?
2 Tell in your own words the story of the shepherds and the angels at the birth of Jesus.
3 What gifts did the wise men give to Jesus? What do you think these gifts stood for?
4 What thoughts does the story of Jesus's birth inspire in people today?
5 Matthew's Gospel several times tells how God communicated with Joseph through dreams. Describe three such occasions, saying in each case what instruction Joseph was given and what action he took.

9 The Child, and the Boy in the Temple of Jerusalem

Story and comments

Eight days after his birth, Jesus was circumcised. And thirty-two days later Mary offered in the Temple a gift to God — two young pigeons. Two old people in the Temple, a man named Simeon and a woman named Anna, seeing Jesus, praised God for him. Simeon called Jesus 'an instrument of salvation' and said he would meet much opposition.

At the age of twelve Jesus was again brought by his parents to the Temple. It was the feast of the Passover. Joseph and Mary set off home, not realising that Jesus had been left behind. Three days later they returned to Jerusalem, anxiously looking for him. They found him in the Temple, talking with the rabbis. Everyone was amazed at his understanding. Mary and Joseph asked why he had done this to them. Jesus answered. 'Did you not know I was bound to be in my father's house?' His parents did not understand this (though Mary remembered it and thought a great deal about it). Jesus returned home and was obedient to his parents. He grew wiser and stronger and was approved of by God and everyone else.

(Luke chapter 2, verses 21 to 52)

1 The circumcision

This was absolutely essential for every Jewish boy, according to the laws of the Old Testament, and had to be done eight days after he was born. This was the moment when a Jewish boy was named. So Joseph and Mary obeyed the angel and called their son Jesus.

2 The presentation

The Jewish law also said that any first-born male child — and

even the first-born male cattle — really belonged to God. To
acknowledge this, forty days after the birth of a first-born male
it was necessary to offer a gift to God in the Temple. Parents,
so to speak, bought back their child from God. Usually they
offered a lamb and a pigeon, but the parents of Jesus were
so poor that they were allowed to offer something less — two
young pigeons. Luke once again stresses the poverty of
Jesus's family.

3 Simeon and Anna

Simeon, Luke says, was waiting for the 'comforting' of Israel.
This 'comforting' was a word used in the Old Testament to
describe the time when God should save his people. Simeon
had also been promised that he would not die until he had
seen the Messiah. Anna, an eighty-four-year-old widow, had
also waited long for this day. Now she began to tell everyone
about Jesus.

So we see in Luke's Gospel that as the parents of Jesus
obey the law of the Old Testament, they find that their child
is *fulfilling* the hopes of the Old Testament as well.

Nunc Dimittis   Simeon's song of praise, now known as the Nunc Dimittis,
later became a famous Christian hymn:

'Lord, now let your servant depart in peace,
according to your word;
for my eyes have seen your salvation,
which you have prepared in the presence of all nations,
a light to shine before non-Jews,
and to glory your people Israel.'

4 Jesus among the rabbis

About the age of twelve a Jewish boy became a 'son of the
law', when he took on himself to be a good Jew. By the time
he was thirteen he would be counted as an adult. The feast
of the Passover celebrated the liberation of the Jews from
Egypt long long ago in the time of Moses. Lambs were
offered in the Jerusalem Temple by each family, and then
eaten later. Jesus and his family travelled the ninety miles
from Nazareth to Jerusalem, almost certainly with a great
company of other visitors. This would make it easy, on the
way back, for Mary and Joseph to think their son was
somewhere else in the large group.

Rabbis as we have seen often taught in the outer courts of the Temple. They would teach by question and answer. They marvelled at Jesus's wisdom. But, the story continues, Jesus increased in wisdom as he grew.

5 Joseph

Joseph is not again mentioned in the Bible after this incident, though Mary makes frequent appearances. Presumably he died before Jesus, at around the age of thirty, began his great public activities. After Joseph's death presumably Jesus took over responsibility for the family — not only his mother but also other relatives (according to Mark chapter 6, verse 3, and Matthew chapter 13, verses 55 and 56).

1 Explain what we mean by 'the presentation in the Temple'.
2 Who sang the 'Nunc Dimittis'? Say what you know about him and his wife.
3 Describe the reaction between Jesus and his mother after he had been temporarily lost in Jerusalem. What might this tell us about problems that can arise between parents and a child growing up?
4 Describe accurately the visit made by Jesus to Jerusalem at the age of twelve.
5 At the age of twelve Jesus visited Jerusalem. What does this tell us about (a) Jewish customs, and (b) Jesus himself?
6 Fill in the missing words:

After three days they found him sitting in the temple surrounded by the teachers, listening to them and putting questions; and all who heard him were amazed at his intelligence and the answers he gave. His parents were astonished to see him there, and his mother said to him, 'My son, why have you treated us like this? Your father and I have been searching for you in great anxiety.' 'What made you search?' he said. 'Did you not know that I was bound to be in my ....?' But they did not understand what he meant. Then he went back with them to ...., and continued to be under their authority.

(Luke chapter 2, verses 46 to 50)

Who are 'they' in the passage?

10 John the Baptist and Jesus

The birth of John the Baptist: story and comments

Zechariah
struck dumb

A priest named Zechariah and his wife Elizabeth had longed for a child, but were now too old. Yet while Zechariah was serving in the Temple, an angel appeared and told him Elizabeth would have a son. They should call the boy John. Zechariah refused to believe it, so the angel (whose name was Gabriel) struck him dumb until the boy was born.

After the baby's birth, the neighbours wished to call him after Zechariah. Zechariah persuaded Elizabeth that they should obey Gabriel and call their son John.

(Luke chapter 1, verses 5 to 25 and 57 to 80)

1 Zechariah

Zechariah was one of twenty thousand men who had the privilege of carrying out duties in the Jerusalem Temple — such as burning incense. He was married to a women who also came from a family of priests.

On one of the twice-yearly occasions when he worked in the Temple the angel appeared to him. The point of his temporary punishment is that he ought to have believed the word of the angel, especially when he learned that this was Gabriel, which means 'the one who stands before God'.

2 John

John means 'God's kind gift'. The whole story emphasises that John was born for a special reason in God's plans.

We learn of John's part in God's plans partly from the angel Gabriel and partly from Zechariah after his speech has come back. The angel says that:

1 John will be great in God's sight.
2 He will not drink wine or strong drink.
3 He will make many Jews come back to their God.
4 He will be filled with God's spirit.
5 Like the prophet Elijah, he will prepare people for their Lord.

NB: it is important to understand who this Lord is. The angel is obviously referring to Malachi chapter 4, verses 5 and 6:

John and Elijah the prophet

'Behold, I will send you Elijah the prophet before the great and terrible day of the Lord comes. And he will turn the hearts of fathers to their children and the hearts of children to their fathers, lest I come and smite the land with a curse.'

The Jews believed that in the last days God would send them a king who would get rid of their enemies, and rule over a sinless nation. They called this king the 'Messiah' (which, as we have seen, is in Greek 'Christ'). Gabriel is telling Zechariah that these last days are approaching and that his son John will play the part of Elijah in announcing all this.

When Zechariah began to speak again he composed a poem, praising God because the Messiah was about to come and because of the role of his son John in this.

He calls John 'the prophet of the Most High', who 'will go before the Lord to prepare his ways.'

3 The main point concerns Jesus

Luke believes that the Lord who is to come, the Messiah, is Jesus. Both the angel Gabriel and Zechariah are saying that John the Baptist will announce that Jesus is the Messiah (or 'the Christ').

John the Baptist announces Jesus as Christ: story and comments

John appeared in the desert. He told people to turn away

from their sins, and he baptised those who agreed to do this. Very many came to him. He was wearing camels' skins, the hairy part on the outside, tied with a leather belt, and he ate locusts and wild honey,

John also said:

'A mightier person than I am comes soon. I am not fit to untie the laces of his sandals. I baptise you with water. He will baptise you with the Holy Spirit.'

(Mark chapter 1, verses 2 to 8)

Compare with this the story as told by:

- Luke chapter 3, verses 1 to 7 and 15 to 17;
- Matthew chapter 3, verses 1 to 6, 11 and 12.

1 When did this happen?

Luke attempts to date this start of Jesus's public life and teaching by saying that John the Baptist appeared in the desert 'in the fifteenth year of the reign of the Emperor Tiberius'. The Emperor Augustus had died and been succeeded by Tiberius in AD 14. So the fifteenth year of Tiberius was AD 28–29.

This is important because Jesus began to teach in Galilee one year later, when John the Baptist was imprisoned. So Jesus stopped being the carpenter's son, looking after his family in Nazareth, in about AD 29. In that year he started the three greatest years of his life on earth. All that we have of his teaching comes from these three years.

2 The hopes of the Old Testament

These hopes are still important here, for Mark, Matthew and Luke. The angel Gabriel had already spoken of John the Baptist's work in terms laid down by the prophet Malachi.

Malachi   Mark here produces another Malachi quotation:

'Behold, I send my messenger to prepare the way before me,'

though Mark mistakenly thinks this statement comes from the prophet Isaiah.

And, since John lived in the desert, Mark and Luke apply

Isaiah

to him part of the prophet Isaiah chapter 40, verse 3:

'The voice of one crying in the wilderness: prepare the way of the Lord; make his paths straight.'

And Luke adds the next two verses from Isaiah:

'Every valley shall be lifted up, and every mountain and hill made low.'

Isaiah's message adapted

But the Gospels have adapted this message. The Old Testament writers, speaking of 'preparing the way of the Lord', were really speaking of preparing *for God*, and for no one else.

John is seen as preparing the way for Jesus, the son of God. (Matthew's Gospel even presents John as using the words of Jesus's own preaching:

'Repent, for the kingdom of heaven is at hand,'

a call later repeated by Jesus.)

3 John's baptism and Jesus's baptism

Just as John claims to be far less important than Jesus, so he says that his baptism is far less important than Jesus's baptism: John's with water, Jesus's with God's spirit.

Matthew and Luke add a strange remark. Jesus, they say, will also baptise people with fire. Here they are stressing that the Messiah will judge between the good and the bad, the way a farmer judges between good and bad corn. He

Baptism by fire

throws the bad corn into the fire.

4 Was John the Baptist a real person?

There is no reason to suppose that John the Baptist was a figment of people's imagination. Other writers, besides the four Gospel-writers, mention him. For instance, Josephus, a Jewish historian, wrote:

'He commanded the Jews to cultivate virtue by behaving with justice towards each other and with piety towards God — and so come to baptism.'

Also, baptising, for which John was most famous, was not part of the usual Old Testament idea of what ought to happen just before the coming of the Messiah. The Gospel-writers must have included this because an historical person — i.e. John — was preaching baptism at the time of Jesus.

Preaching of baptism

We can probably take as historical facts that John the Baptist wore the skins of camels, and lived off honey from wild bees as well as locusts (which were either boiled alive before being eaten, or roasted in a fire).

John the Baptist's own message: story and comments

When John saw many Pharisees and Sadducees coming to be baptised, he turned on them and said they were a brood of vipers. They thought they would escape from 'the wrath to come' because they were descended from Abraham. But what was needed was good fruit. Otherwise they would be chopped down like trees bearing bad fruit.

(Matthew chapter 3, verses 7 to 10)

This teaching, according to Luke's Gospel, is addressed to everyone, not just Pharisees and Sadducees. Luke adds that John said:

- Give generously to those poorer than you are.
- If you are a tax collector, only take what is right.
- If you are a soldier, be content with your pay. Do not force money out of people.

(Luke chapter 3, verses 11 to 14)

1 Whom is he addressing?

No doubt John said these things more than once. Matthew has specified Pharisees and Sadducees because he is especially interested in addressing his Gospel to the Jews. Luke talks about *everyone* because his Gospel goes beyond the boundaries of Judaism. But he still quotes John the Baptist using Old Testament phrases — such as 'the wrath to come' — which only Jews would understand. The wrath to come referred to the punishment of the wicked at the Last Judgment by God.

2 Insults

John has a fine insult for those who hope to be saved simply because they are descended from Abraham: God can make sons of Abraham out of stones. There is a pun here. In Aramaic 'sons' and 'stones' are almost the same word.

Stones
Snakes

He compares them to vipers. Snakes have been regarded as evil beings since the story of Adam and Eve in the book of Genesis (read Genesis chapter 3, verses 1 to 15).

3 Preaching

As we have seen, John's preaching is often very like (if not exactly the same as) the teaching of Jesus. His attack on the Pharisees and the Sadducees mirrors the later attacks of Jesus. By contrast with this, the special teaching given only by Luke seems so banal that some readers have concluded Luke had his own reason for including it: he wanted to show how much more exciting and original was the teaching of Jesus.

Banality in
Luke

1 Give an account of the announcement by Zechariah of the birth of John the Baptist. What is the main point of this story?
2 John the Baptist is called 'the prophet of the most high'. What does this mean? What does the angel tell Zechariah about John?
3 Describe John the Baptist's appearance in the desert. What did he say about Jesus and what did he tell the Jews to do?
4 What was John the Baptist's attitude towards Pharisees and Sadducees? What did he say about them? What do you think John the Baptist would say to us today?

John baptises Jesus: story and comments

Mark

Jesus came from Nazareth and John baptised him in the river Jordan. As he was coming up out of the water, he saw the heavens immediately opened. He saw God's spirit

The Baptism, a
mosaic in
Ravenna, Italy

descending on him. It looked like a dove. A voice came from
heaven, saying:

> 'You are my beloved son. I am well pleased with you.'
>
> (Mark chapter 1, verses 9 to 11)

Matthew   Matthew adds:

> 'John would have stopped Jesus, saying "I need to be
> baptised by you." Jesus answered, "Let it happen; it is
> correct for me to fulfil everything that is right."'
>
> (Matthew chapter 3, verses 13 to 17)

Luke	In Luke the story is the same as Mark's, save that Jesus is praying when the Holy Spirit comes from heaven.

(Luke chapter 3, verses 21 and 22)

John	John tells us:

> that John the Baptist claimed to have seen the Holy Spirit descend on Jesus, like a dove.

(John chapter 1, verses 31 to 34)

1 Why a dove?

The Jews believed that when God made the world his spirit flew over it like a dove. Now that same spirit was descending on Jesus, to make a better world.

2 Why do the heavens open?

Mark gives us a clue by using an unusual word in Greek which means 'split open' or 'rent open'. This is a word he has taken from the Greek translation of Isaiah chapter 64, verse 1 — a prayer to God which cries, 'O that you would split the heavens and come down!' At last, Mark is saying, this has happened. God has come to help his people — but through Jesus.

3 What does the voice from heaven mean?

There are several hidden signposts to verses of the Old Testament in the words from heaven.
  Psalm 2, verse 7, reads:

> 'You are my son; today I have begotten you.'

	This Psalm had been used at coronations. The idea was that God would treat the king as his own son. After the Jews ceased to have kings, they decided that this verse pointed to the coming Messiah. So the voice from heaven points to
King/Messiah	Jesus as the Messiah, and as the new king of the Jews.
Isaiah chapter 42, verse 1, reads:

> 'Behold my servant, whom I uphold,
> my chosen, in whom my soul delights.'

Suffering servant	The voice from heaven claims that Jesus is God's servant, for God is pleased with him. But the servant in Isaiah's mind has

a difficult task. He is to suffer for other people. Here in the story of his baptism Jesus is already on the way to his crucifixion.

Beloved son

The voice calls Jesus 'my beloved son'. God uses that word 'beloved' of the son of Abraham — Abraham was the ancient father of the Jews — just as Abraham's son is to be killed. Here is another hint of the crucifixion.

4 Why, in the earlier stories, does only Jesus see the dove?

On the other hand, in John, for instance, the Baptist also sees it. Is the answer to do with Mark's idea of the Messianic secret (which we have already discussed)? Mark wants everyone to know that Jesus is the son of God — that is why he wrote his Gospel. But he also had to find some way of explaining why many people never spotted this when Jesus lived in Palestine.

Messianic secret

John's Gospel does not try to answer this question, so he has no problems in supposing that others besides Jesus saw the dove.

5 Why was Jesus baptised at all?

This problem puzzled the early Christians who regarded Jesus as sinless. He did not need to repent and be baptised. Matthew — showing John the Baptist trying to stop Jesus being baptised — reveals that this question troubles him too.

Later Christians have suggested that Jesus wanted to show that he approved of what John the Baptist was doing. He approved of John's message. Also, he wanted to give people an example — they too needed to repent and be baptised.

Others have seen the baptism of Jesus as a moment when he came to realise fully who he was and what God demanded of him. This may easily be reading too much into the four accounts of the baptism. Even so, they do set out who Jesus was very clearly; and, for the first time publicly, Jesus appears as John's successor.

How do Jesus and the Baptist relate to each other? Story and comments

According to Matthew

Herod put John the Baptist in prison. There John heard of the activities of Jesus. He sent his followers to Jesus to ask:

'Are you the Messiah, or must we look for someone else?'

Jesus replied that because of his activities:

the blind can see;
the lame can walk;
lepers are healed;
the deaf can hear;
the dead are raised;
good news is preached to the poor.

When John's followers have gone away, Jesus speaks to the crowd about the Baptist. He says he is a prophet and 'more than a prophet'. About him, says Jesus, the prophet Malachi wrote:

'Behold, I send my messenger before your face, who shall prepare your way before you.'

Then Jesus made his own judgment about John the Baptist:

'Among those born of women there has risen no one greater than John the Baptist; yet he who is least in the kingdom of heaven is greater than he.'

Jesus added:

'If you are willing to accept it, he is Elijah'

(Matthew chapter 11, verses 2 to 14)

Luke's version

Luke's Gospel tells the same story, though Luke does not quote Jesus's statement that John the Baptist is Elijah come again. As in Matthew, Jesus draws attention to a difference between himself and John the Baptist:

'John the Baptist has come eating no bread and drinking no wine; and you say, "He has a demon." The son of man has come eating and drinking; and you say, "Behold a glutton and a drunkard, a friend of tax collectors and sinners".'

(Luke chapter 7, verses 18 to 34)

1 The Messiah

Both Gospels here represent Jesus claiming to be the
Messiah, in response to John's question. Jesus refers to these
miracles for two reasons:

1 He has performed them all in the previous days of his
   ministry (and all are described in the previous chapters of
   Matthew and Luke).
2 They are all (except cleansing lepers) said by the Old
   Testament prophet Isaiah to be miracles that will happen
   when the Messiah comes.

2 The messenger

Both Gospels now quote the verse of Malachi used earlier by
Mark of John the Baptist. He is the messenger who prepares
the way for the Lord — that is, for Jesus. John (Matthew
emphasises, and Luke reluctantly agrees) is greater than any
other human being, but in no way as great as Jesus or as
anyone who now follows Jesus.

3 Elijah

John the Baptist plays the role of Elijah, who, according to the
Old Testament, was to return to announce the coming of the
Messiah Luke elsewhere (chapter 16, verse 16) expresses
the difference between the era of John the Baptist and his
own era: 'The law and the prophets continued until John;
since then is preached the good news of the kingdom of
God.'

4 Jesus and the Baptist compared

Both Gospels — Matthew and Luke — compare the pattern
of life followed by John the Baptist with that followed by Jesus
(one fasted and did not drink; one ate well and did drink).
Neither was praised for his way of life. Jesus was also
criticised because of his friendship with tax-collectors and
sinners.

Jesus believed that he and his followers ought to rejoice:
they should rejoice simply because he, who brought the
good news, was with them.

In these four ways, then, Jesus makes clear that in spite of his great regard for John the Baptist, their relationship is that of the messenger of the Messiah and the Messiah himself.

The death of John the Baptist: story and comments

King Herod was persuaded by his wife Herodias to throw John the Baptist in prison, since John had criticised both of them for marrying. (Herodias had formerly been married to Herod's brother.) But Herod was afraid of John. He knew John led a good life, and therefore would not kill him.

On his birthday Herod gave a feast. Herodias's daughter danced for him and his guests. He was so pleased that he vowed to give her whatever she asked — 'even half my kingdom'. Her mother told her to ask for the head of John the Baptist on a plate. In front of his guests, Herod did not dare refuse. John was beheaded. His head was given to the dancer. She gave it to her mother. Then John's followers buried his body. They told Jesus about this.

(Mark chapter 6, verses 14 to 29;
Matthew chapter 14, verses 1 to 12)

1 Who was Herod?

The Herod in question was a son of Herod the Great, known as Herod Antipas. He was not strictly a king (as Mark wrongly calls him) but a 'tetrarch' (as Matthew rightly calls him). Herod comes out of the story better than his wife or her daughter, though he still appears as a weak man. The fact that he killed John the Baptist is confirmed by the Jewish historian Josephus.

2 The fates of Jesus and the Baptist compared

Herod's fear of Jesus

This story slightly concerns the relationship of Jesus and the Baptist. Herod, perhaps like many others, for a time feared that Jesus was John the Baptist come to life again. This points to the initial closeness of the teachings of both men, as well as to the fact that both of them baptised followers (read on this John's Gospel, chapter 3, verses 22 to 24).

The fate of John the Baptist also emphasises the danger

under which Jesus taught and worked. Jesus was obviously aware of this. Mark's Gospel reveals that after John had been executed, Jesus for a time deliberately moved out of the reach of Herod Antipas, working in Bethsaida, Tyre and Sidon, Decapolis and Caesarea Philippi.

Matthew's Gospel is especially quick to parallel the fates of Jesus and John the Baptist. In Matthew chapter 17, verse 12, Jesus says that just as people have ill-treated the Baptist, 'so also the son of man will suffer at their hands'.

1 'Jesus came from Nazareth in Galilee and was baptised in the Jordan by John. At the moment when he came up out of the water, he saw the heavens torn open and the Spirit, like a dove, descending upon him. And a voice spoke from heaven: "Thou art my Son, my Beloved; on thee my favour rests".' (Mark chapter 1, verses 9 to 11, New English Bible version).
Why a dove? Why do the heavens open? What does the voice from heaven mean?
2 Why do you think Jesus was baptised? Why did his baptism trouble the early Christians?
3 Christians are still baptised today. Say what meaning you think this ceremony has for them.
4 In what ways did John the Baptist's message differ from the message of Jesus?
5 What did Jesus admire in John the Baptist? Illustrate your answer with quotations.
6 Relate the story of the imprisonment and execution of John the Baptist. What does this account reveal about the characters of Herod, Herod's wife and John himself?
7 'Get away from here, for Herod wants to kill you.' Who brought this warning to Jesus? What did Jesus call Herod?

11   The Temptations of Jesus

Jesus in the desert: story and comments

The Holy Spirit led Jesus into the desert. For forty days and nights he ate nothing. The devil came to him, with three temptations:

1 Jesus was hungry. The devil said to him:
    'If you are the son of God, turn these stones into loaves of bread.'
    Jesus replied:
    'We should live not by bread alone, but by every word of God.'
2 The devil took him to Jerusalem, set him high up on the Temple walls, and said:
    'If you are the son of God, throw yourself to the ground. The Scriptures say God will send his angels to save you.'
    Jesus replied:
    'You shall not tempt the Lord your God.'
3 The devil took Jesus to a very high mountain. He could see every kingdom in the world. The devil said:
    'I will give you all these, if you will worship me.'
    Jesus replied:
    'Go away, Satan! You shall worship the Lord your God, and serve only him.'

The devil went away. Angels then came to care for Jesus.

(Mark chapter 1, verses 12 and 13;
Matthew chapter 4, verses 1 to 11;
Luke chapter 4, verses 1 to 13)

*Christ in the
Wilderness:
Rising from
Sleep in the
Morning* by
Stanley
Spencer

1 Quotations from the Old Testament

The devil quotes the Scriptures to Jesus — Psalm 91, verses
11 and 12 — about how God's angels will care for Jesus.

Law of Moses   In reply Jesus three times quotes the law of Moses, in the
book of Deuteronomy:

* chapter 8, verse 3;
* chapter 6, verse 16;
* chapter 6, verse 13.

2 The deeper meaning of the temptations

Jesus is contemplating how to carry out his future task of
bringing the truth to mankind. How is he to bring to earth the
kingdom of God? He rejects three false ways:

**Three false
ways**

1 to appeal to men and women by offering them material
things — bread, made from stones — thus appealing to
their selfish natures;

2 to appeal to miraculous tricks, as if men and women need not work for the kingdom of God in response to the good news of God's love for them;

3 to make concessions to evil in order to gain 'the kingdoms of the world'.

3 Mark's Gospel is different

In two verses Mark simply says that Jesus was in the wilderness. Mark says four things happened there:

1 Jesus stayed forty days;
2 he was tempted by the devil;
3 he was with wild beasts;
4 angels cared for him.

The temptations were clearly greatly thought about later. Mark is simply describing a period of quiet and withdrawal before Jesus takes on his great work. But (as D E Nineham wrote in his commentary, *Saint Mark*) Mark shows here that Jesus's subsequent ministry — and the life of the early church — was carrying on and completing 'a decisive battle with the powers of evil successfully begun before ever the ministry opened'.

4 The battle with the devil is not over

Luke especially stresses this, in chapter 4, verse 13:

'And when the devil had finished every temptation, he left Jesus — *till another time.*'

1 'We should not live by bread alone,' said Jesus. What does 'living by bread alone' mean for us today? What else ought we to live by?

2 Give an account of Jesus's three temptations and say how they represent three false ways of carrying out his future work.

3 What four things does Mark's Gospel say happened to Jesus in the wilderness?

4 Name some modern temptations, and say why they must be rejected.

12   The Twelve Apostles

Choosing disciples: story and comments

Simon and Andrew

Jesus walked by the sea of Galilee and saw a man named Simon with his brother Andrew about to cast a fishing net in the water. They were fishermen by trade. Jesus said, 'Follow me and I will make you into fishers of men.' They left their nets and went with him. A little further on he saw two other

James and John

brothers, James and John. They too were fishermen. They were sitting in their boat, mending their nets. Jesus called on them to follow him; so they left their father Zebedee and his hired hands in the boat and went with Jesus.

(Mark chapter 1, verses 16 to 22;
Matthew chapter 4, verses 18 to 20)

Levi

Jesus next saw a man named Levi, a tax collector, and said to him, 'Follow me.' Levi first made him a great feast in his home. Matthew's Gospel tells us Levi was called Matthew.

(Mark chapter 2, verse 14;
Matthew chapter 9, verse 9;
Luke chapter 5, verses 27 to 29)

The twelve

Finally Jesus made the number up to twelve. These were: Simon, whom he surnamed Peter; James and John, whom he surnamed Boanerges (meaning 'Sons of Thunder'); Andrew; Philip; Bartholomew; Matthew; Thomas; James the son of Alphaeus; Thaddaeus; Simon the Zealot; and Judas Iscariot, who later betrayed Jesus.

(Mark chapter 3, verses 13 to 19;
Matthew chapter 10, verses 1 to 4;
Luke chapter 6, verses 12 to 16)

1 The number twelve

This has great importance in view of the fact that the Jews

were formed originally into twelve tribes. In Matthew
chapter 19, verse 28, Jesus gives them special roles in the
new kingdom of Israel which he is starting:

> 'Truly, I say to you, in the new world, when the son of man
> shall sit on his glorious throne, you who have followed me
> will also sit on twelve thrones, judging the twelve tribes of
> Israel.'

So these twelve men are the equivalents of Jacob's twelve
sons who (according to the Old Testament) gave their names
to the twelve tribes of Israel.

2 Some vagueness

The twelve names given on page 100 above vary elsewhere
in the New Testament. And John's Gospel lists among the
disciples other names. Probably the selection of the twelve
took place in a more haphazard fashion than the Gospels
relate. Luke adds an even more formal note: that Jesus
prayed before selecting his twelve leaders. But the truth was
probably far less tidy than this. John chapter 1, verses 35 to
51, reveals that Andrew and Simon had once been disciples
of John the Baptist before joining with Jesus.

Inner circle   An inner circle of the twelve soon developed — disciples
closest to Jesus. These were Peter (formerly Simon), James
and John, who sometimes went with Jesus when the others
were left behind.

Teaching the twelve Apostles: story and comments

Jesus told his Sermon on the Plain to his twelve Apostles and
'a great multitude' (Luke chapter 6, verses 17 to 49). But the
parallel passage in Matthew (chapters 5 to 7), the Sermon on
the Mount, was addressed solely to his closest disciples.

Later Jesus decided that his twelve Apostles ought to
share in his own work, even to the extent of performing the
same miracles as he did. In a great discourse, Jesus tells
them he is to send them out as sheep among wolves. They
will be:

Persecution   delivered up to local Jewish councils;
dragged before governors;

dragged before kings;
hated, because people also hate Jesus;
persecuted in towns.

But they are not to worry. If they are persecuted in one town, leave it and go to the next. Don't fear those who can destroy the body; fear those who can harm the soul.

Jesus tells them that those who receive the Apostles will be in effect receiving Jesus; those who feed them or give them drink will be doing this for Jesus too. They were not to take much wealth with them. He says:

'have power over unclean spirits and cast them out of people;
heal the sick;

Healing power   heal every infirmity.'

(Matthew chapter 10)

This section obviously has in mind — as well as Jesus's twelve Apostles — those who were to carry out Jesus's mission after he had been crucified, risen and ascended to heaven. The sufferings Jesus predicted were those undergone by members of the early church, including the circle around the Gospel-writer himself.

An Apostle must be totally committed: story and comments

Jesus told his Apostles:

'Whoever loves father or mother more than me is not worthy of me; and whoever loves son or daughter more than me is not worthy of me. And whoever does not take up his cross and follow me is not worthy of me. He who finds his life will lose it, and he who loses his life for my sake will find it.'

(Matthew chapter 10, verses 37 to 39;
Luke chapter 14, verses 25 to 27)

Once a rich young man asked Jesus what he needed to do to gain eternal life. Jesus repeated to him the Old Testament law, adding:

'If you want to be perfect, sell everything you have and give to the poor; then you will have treasure in heaven. After that, come and follow me.' The rich man went away.

Jesus said to his followers:

> 'It will be hard for a rich man to enter the kingdom of heaven. It is easier for a camel to go through the eye of a needle than for a rich man to enter the kingdom of God.'

But he added:

> 'Every one who has left houses or brothers or sisters or mother or children or lands for my sake, will receive a hundred times as much, and inherit eternal life.'
>
> (Matthew chapter 19, verses 16 to 29)

1 Taking up a cross

There is such an obvious reference in this to the crucifixion that the story has probably been modified to include this sentence. But it properly sums up what Jesus is saying to his followers about the difficulties (and rewards) of imitating him.

2 The disciples often failed Jesus

These difficulties inevitably meant that they would. Peter, under stress, was to deny he knew Jesus. Judas betrayed him. These two men come at the beginning and end of the list of Jesus's twelve Apostles, see 'Choosing disciples', page 100.

1 Jesus chose twelve Apostles. Say why you think he chose that number. What were they to do in the new world Jesus was bringing? Name the ones closest to Jesus.
2 Jesus said that his disciples would suffer. Give three examples of what he said would happen to them.
3 How might a follower of Jesus suffer today? Write about other groups of people (besides Christians) who suffer for their beliefs in the world today. Do you know any words of Jesus that might help them?
4 Say what Jesus told his followers about 'taking up a cross'. What did he mean? What 'crosses' do people have to take up today?
5 'Do not be afraid. From now on you will be catching men.' To whom did Jesus say this? Why did he use the phrase 'catching men'? What did he mean by it?

6 Fill in the missing words:

'If you wish to go the whole way, go, sell your possessions, and give to the ...., and then you will have riches in ....; and come, follow me.' When the young man heard this, he went away with a heavy heart; for he was a man of great wealth.

Jesus said to his disciples, 'I tell you this: a rich man will find it hard to enter the kingdom of .... I repeat, it is easier for a .... to pass through the eye of a .... than for a rich man to enter the kingdom of God.' The disciples were amazed to hear this. 'Then who can be saved?' they asked. Jesus looked them in the face, and said. 'For men this is impossible; but everything is possible for God.'

At this Peter said, 'Here are we who left everything to become your followers. What will there be for us?' Jesus replied, 'I tell you this: in the world that is to be, when the Son of Man is seated on his throne in heavenly splendour, you my followers will have thrones of your own, where you will sit as judges of the twelve tribes of Israel. And anyone who has left brothers or sisters, father, mother, or children, land or houses for the sake of my name will be repaid many times over, and gain .... life.

(Matthew chapter 19, verses 22 to 29)

Do you agree with Jesus's attitude to riches? Give reasons why you agree or disagree.

13 The Sermon on the Mount

The Beatitudes: story and comments

Jesus took his disciples away from the crowds, up a mountain. He sat down and said:

> 'Blessed are the poor in spirit, for theirs is the kingdom of heaven.
> Blessed are those who mourn, for they shall be comforted.
> Blessed are the meek for they shall inherit the earth.
> Blessed are those who hunger and thirst after righteousness, for they shall be satisfied.
> Blessed are the merciful, for they shall obtain mercy.
> Blessed are the pure in heart, for they shall see God.
> Blessed are the peacemakers, for they shall be called the sons of God.
> Blessed are those who are persecuted for righteousness' sake, for theirs is the kingdom of heaven.
> Blessed are you when men revile you and persecute you and say all kinds of evil against you falsely on my account. Rejoice and be glad, for your reward is great in heaven for so people persecuted the prophets who were before you.'
> (Matthew chapter 5, verses 1 to 12)

1 The Sermon on the Mount is about happiness

However, the 'Beatitudes' show that Jesus has a most unusual view about what makes one happy. ('Beatitude' comes from the Latin for 'blessed'.)

Those who will find happiness are for the most part the exact opposite of those most people think happy. They are:

the poor,
the meek,

those who are mourning;
those who are hungry and thirsty (for righteousness),
those are who are persecuted (for the sake of
righteousness).

In addition Jesus suggests that qualities not normally
supposed to lead to worldly success will lead even so to
happiness. These qualities are:

to be pure in heart,
to make peace,
to be merciful.

In short, Jesus has turned upside down what most people
imagine will lead to happiness. You will not find happiness,
he is saying, by trampling on others, by seeking great
wealth, by looking after your own self — right or wrong.

2 The Sermon on the Plain

The Sermon on the Mount needs to be compared with the
Sermon on the Plain (in Luke, chapter 6, verses 17 to 26). It
then becomes clear that these sayings of Jesus have been
arranged by each Gospel-writer. Luke makes the four
Beatitudes that he uses even sharper than does Matthew:

'Blessed are you poor, for yours is the kingdom of God.
Blessed are you that hunger now, for you shall be satisfied.
Blessed are you that weep now, for you shall laugh.
Blessed are you when men hate you, and when they
exclude you and revile you, and cast out your name as
evil, on account of the son of man. Rejoice in that day, and
leap for joy, for behold, your reward is great in heaven; for
so their fathers did to the prophets.'

Notice what Luke excludes. For instance he writes,
'Blessed are you poor,' whereas Matthew writes, 'Blessed are
the poor *in spirit.*' Luke writes, 'Blessed are you that hunger
now,' whereas Matthew writes, 'Blessed are those who
hunger and thirst *after righteousness.*' Is Matthew perhaps

Does Matthew water down?

watering down what Jesus said? Does he find Jesus's words
too strong for him or his readers (or had this watering down
been done before Matthew learned the Beatitudes)?
Luke also reinforces the power of the Beatitudes by 'woes'
or 'curses':

Cursed are the rich; cursed are those who are full now;

cursed are you that laugh now; cursed are you when all men speak well of you.

3 The relevance of the Beatitudes

Luke's continual insistence on the word 'you' hints that he meant Jesus's words to apply to those who were reading his Gospel as well as to Jesus's disciples. Matthew's Sermon on the Mount makes this even clearer. After saying 'Blessed are those . . .' many times, suddenly Jesus says:

'Blessed are *you* when men revile you and persecute you . . .' Both Matthew and Luke were writing at a time when Christians were being increasingly persecuted.

The relevance of these words *today* should not go unnoticed. Men and women of honour and ideals are still being persecuted, in very many parts of the world. Does the Sermon on the Mount mean that they should simply accept persecution (or hunger, or poverty) in this world — hoping for better things in the next world? Or is there also implied the notion that those who are responsible for persecution (hunger, poverty, and so on) are condemned by God and need to be opposed by God's followers?

Jesus talks about the law and the prophets: summary and comments

Jesus now says: 'Do not think that I have come to abolish the law and the prophets. I have come not to abolish them but to fulfil them.' He argues 'No part of God's commandments can be set aside. But you must do even more. Your righteousness must be greater than the righteousness of the scribes and the Pharisees.'

To understand what this means, consider:

1 Murder
   The law says, 'You shall not kill.'
   Jesus says, 'Whoever is angry with his brother should be judged; whoever is angry with his brother ought to come before the courts;
   whoever calls his brother a fool is in danger of hell-fire.

Do not dare to try to worship God — 'offering a gift at the altar' — until you have made friends with your brother.

2 Adultery
The law says, 'You shall not commit adultery.'
Jesus says, 'Even to look at a woman lustfully is to commit adultery in your heart.'
Pluck out your eye and throw it away, rather than let it offend you.

3 Divorce
The law says you may give your wife a certificate telling her you have divorced her. Jesus says that unless you do this because *she* is unchaste, you are wrong. Even to marry a divorced women is to commit adultery.

4 Swearing oaths
The law says you should perform faithfully anything you have promised on oath. Jesus says you need not take an oath at all; for your word shall *always* be trustworthy.

5 Justice
The law says, 'An eye for an eye and a tooth for a tooth.'
Jesus says that you should not even resist an evil person. If you are hit on one cheek, let them hit you on the other as well. If somebody wants to take your cloak, give him your overcoat as well. When you are forced to travel one mile with someone, go two miles with him.

6 Love and hatred
The law says, 'Love your neighbours and hate your enemies.'
Jesus says, 'Love your enemies. Pray for those who persecute you.' God loves everyone — the sun shines and the rain falls on good and bad alike. That is perfection. You must be perfect as God is perfect.

(Matthew chapter 5, verses 17 to 48)

1 The law

In all six instances from the law, Jesus is quoting the Old Testament. He is summarising much material — not just the Ten Commandments in Exodus chapter 20, but also sayings attributed to Moses. It's worth nothing that the Old Testament says 'Love your neighbours' (Leviticus chapter 19, verse

18), but does not add 'Hate your enemies'. People assume
that loving friends means hating enemies.

2 Jesus

**The law must
stand**

In each case (save one), Jesus says that the Old Testament
law needs to stand. But he demands *much more.*

**Positive actions
count**

He also insists that positive actions count in the law. Don't
wait for people to ask. 'Make friends with your accuser,'
'Give to him who begs from you,' 'Pray for those who
persecute you.'

**Spirit of the
law**

Jesus also wants his disciples to look to the spirit of the
law. Take, for instance, oath-taking. When the law insists that
people must keep promises made on oath, it does *not* imply
that any other promise can be broken!

3 Scribes and Pharisees

The scribes (or 'Doctors of the Law') had studied the law
more than any other group in Jewish society. The Pharisees,
in their intense desire to obey the law, never ceased to
develop more and more complex interpretations of it, laying
down the law for every act in minute detail.

Jesus was often at odds with them. But here he in no way
condemns their passionate devotion to the law. On the
contrary, he says to his followers, 'Unless your righteousness
exceeds that of the scribes and Pharisees, you will never
enter the kingdom of heaven.'

4 Authority

Note here the very last verses of the Sermon on the Mount:

'And when Jesus had finished these sayings, the crowds
were astonished at his teaching, for hhe taught them as
one who had authority, and not as the scribes.'
(Matthew chapter 7, verses 28 and 29)

The law of the Old Testament did not come from Moses or
from another human being; the words of the prophets were
not presented as their own words; they spoke the words of
God. The law was God's law.

Now Jesus comes saying, 'You have heard that it was said
. . . but I say to you.' He is not simply learning all about the
law and setting it out in detail, as these famous, venerated

scribes did. They still relied on the authority of the law itself, not on their own authority.

Jesus relies on his own authority. If the law came from God and Jesus dares set it out in its innermost truth on his own authority, what kind of claim is Jesus making for himself?

No wonder those who heard him were astonished.

Our inner motives: summary and comments

Jesus then said, 'Be careful that you do not behave righteously only where people can see you; for then you will have no reward from your father in heaven.'
He gave three examples:

1 Almsgiving
Hypocrites, when they give alms in the synagogue, sound a trumpet, so that people will praise them. Well, that is their reward; nothing more.

When *you* give alms, Jesus continued, do this so secretly that even your left hand does not know what your right hand is giving. Your heavenly father will know, and will reward you.

2 Prayer
Hypocrites love to stand and pray in synagogues and at street corners, so that people may see them. Well, that is their reward; nothing more.

When *you* pray, Jesus continued, go into your inner room, shut the door, and pray to your father in secret. Your heavenly father will reward you.

3 Fasting
Hypocrites, when they fast, deliberately look miserable, so that people will know they are fasting. Well, that is their reward; nothing more.

When *you* fast, Jesus continued, make sure there is no change in your normal appearance. ('Wash your face and anoint your head.') Fast for your heavenly father in secret. He will reward you.

(Matthew chapter 6, verses 1 to 6)

1 Scribes and Pharisees

Jesus is here still showing how one's righteousness must exceed that of the scribes and Pharisees. The Pharisees, especially, had by the time of Jesus worked out that of the

Giving alms ways to God's favour, giving alms, praying (apart from the usual worship of the Temple and the synagogues) and fasting were the three most important.

Often those who gave a great deal were offered the best seats in the synagogues. So they were rewarded by their fellow-men.

Praying By the time of Jesus it was usual for a godly person to pray at least twice a day: in the morning at around 9 a.m.; in the afternoon at around 3 p.m. Some said there was extra merit if you went to pray in the synagogue.

Fasting The rules for fasting had also been worked out; usually it made a man look bizarre. Men did not comb their beards. Sometimes they did not even wash. Frequently they put cold ashes on their heads.

2 The motive must be right

Jesus does not disagree at all with the three ways of finding favour with God. To give alms, to pray privately, to fast, all trained a person in godliness. But the motive had to be right. The only way to avoid doing these godly acts in order to reap praise from men rather than God was to perform them in secret.

Anxiety: summary and comments

1 No need for treasures on earth

Treasure in heaven Jesus says that in any case they cannot last. Moths eat clothing. Metals rust. Thieves steal your goods. You need treasures in heaven. Remember, he warns, 'Where your treasure is, there will your heart be also.'

2 Whom do you serve?

God and mammon God or your possessions? Jesus pointed out that a servant cannot obey two masters. Their orders will conflict. The servant will have to decide which master he loves and which he hates. So, 'You cannot serve God and mammon.

3 Seek God's kingdom

The future Birds, said Jesus, don't worry about the future. They rely on God to feed them.

Flowers, he continued, don't worry about the future. God clothes them beautifully.

You are much more valuable to God than birds or flowers. So why do you worry about food, drink or clothing. God knows you need all these.

'Seek first the kingdom of God and God's righteousness. All the rest shall be yours as well.'

Do not be anxious for tomorrow, says Jesus; simply live facing today's problems.

(Matthew chapter 6, verses 19 to 34)

1 Treasures in heaven

As we have already seen in the Sermon on the Mount, they are brought about by truly (secretly) worshipping God by alms-giving, fasting and prayer.

2 You cannot obey two masters

Just as people can give alms, fast and pray — but not for the sake of God, only to gain glory from other people — so men and women can pretend to be serving God while serving mammon ('Mammon' is Aramaic for 'possessions'.) The idea, says Jesus, is as ridiculous as a servant trying to obey two masters who give contradictory orders. Either you love God, or you love your earthly possessions. You cannot love both.

3 What's the use of worrying?

This passage is found also in Luke (chapter 12, verses 22 to 34). It was obviously very important for the first Christians, who left everything and followed Jesus. Does it have a wider importance, for others as well?

Certainly it is true that we have very limited control over our lives. Jesus does not seem to be saying, 'Care about nothing at all.' We are to take some thought for today: what we have to do, how we shall live, what we shall eat. Being anxious about *tomorrow*, he says, is pointless. Wait till it comes. Then cope with it.

Even more important than this is Jesus's insistence that there is more than this world to be concerned about. What

Seek the kingdom of God

counts is our commitment to doing God's will: to seeking the kingdom of God. We shall only seek his kingdom if we trust him. So, says Jesus, trust God to provide your earthly needs as well.

How to treat others: summary and comments

The way in which you judge others is the way you will be judged, Jesus says.

What hypocrisy people reveal! They see a stiny splinter in another person's eye; they never notice a log in their own eye. See to the huge log in your own eye before you try to remove the splinter from your brother's eye.

(Matthew chapter 7, verses 1 to 5)

Jesus added: 'Whatever you wish people to do to you, do to them; or this is the law and the prophets.'

(Matthew chapter 7, verse 12)

1 Fulfilling the Jewish law

In these two passages Jesus himself is teaching like a rabbi, adapting the sayings that were current among the Jews of his day. In this way he is still insisting that he is not destroying the Jewish law but fulfilling it.

We even know that the saying about the splinter and the log in two people's eyes was said by other Jewish rabbis. Jesus applies it to the way God treats us. We have already been told to be perfect—as God is perfect. Part of God's greatness, in Jesus's teaching, is that he is merciful. So must we be.

2 The Golden Rule

The command in Matthew chapter 7, verse 12, we now call the Golden Rule. It has a long history in Jewish thought:

> The book of Tobit said: 'What you yourself hate, do not do to anyone else.'
> A famous rabbi named Hillel, asked to recite the whole law standing on one leg, said quickly, 'What you do not want others to do to you, do not do to them.'

Jesus takes both these *negative* rules and makes them *positive*: 'Whatever you wish people to do to you, do to them.'

14   The Lord's Prayer

The prayer: story and comments

Our Father who art in heaven	Father,
Hallowed be your name.	Hallowed be your name.
Your kingdom come.	Your kingdom come.
Your will be done on earth as it is in heaven.	
Give us this day our daily bread.	Give us each day our daily bread.
And forgive us our debts, as we also have forgiven our debtors.	And forgive us our sins, for we also forgive everyone who is indebted to us.
And lead us not into temptation, but deliver us from evil.	And let us not fall into temptation.
(Matthew chapter 6, verses 9 to 13)	(Luke chapter 11, verses 2 to 4)

1 The two versions

Matthew

Matthew gives his version of the Lord's Prayer in the middle of the Sermon on the Mount.

Luke

Luke's version does not appear in the Sermon on the Plain, but later, when the disciples — seeing Jesus praying — ask him to teach them how to do this.

The two prayers are recognisably the same, but scholars guess:

that Matthew's, being much longer, is a later developed form;

that Luke's is the form in which missionaries carried the prayer to the Gentiles.

2 The context of Matthew's version

Jesus has been speaking about the self-centred way in which
some people pray publicly, so as to be rewarded by man's
praise, not God's. He adds that some non-Jews (Gentiles)
think God will be more likely to hear them if they gabble on
and on and on. Jesus here gives them the Lord's Prayer as an
example of how, in one brief prayer, you can say all you
need to God. And indeed this prayer is much shorter than
most other ancient Jewish prayers.

3 The context of Luke's version

Jesus, asked to teach his disciples to pray, gives them the
model for every Christian prayer.

Luke also adds a parable about the man who knocks and
knocks on a friend's door at midnight, until at last the friend
opens up. We are to continue praying, even if we get no
immediate answer. 'Ask, and it will be given you,' says
Jesus here.

In addition Luke adds the question whether any father
would give evil gifts to his children — a serpent instead of a
fish; a scorpion instead of an egg. We have a father in
heaven who also gives good gifts to his children.

4 Luke and Matthew — the difference

Luke (says the scholar Joachim Jeremias in his book *The
Prayers of Jesus*) offers the Lord's Prayer 'to people who
must for the first time learn to pray and whose courage to
pray must be roused'.

Matthew offers the Lord's Prayer 'to people who have
learned to pray in childhood but whose prayer stands in
danger of becoming routine'.

1 Write down in your own words *five* of the Beatitudes.
   Who are those expected by Jesus to find happiness? Why
   is his choice strange?
2 Luke's Gospel adds to the Beatitudes, curses. Who are
   the people who are cursed?
3 Jesus said that people are blessed when they are
   persecuted for his sake. Do you know of anyone being

persecuted today? Could they in any way be described as blessed?

4 Is it foolish to love your enemies?

5 Fill in the missing words:

How blest are those who know that they are ....;
   the kingdom of Heaven is theirs.
How blest are the ....;
   they shall find consolation.
How blest are those of a .... spirit;
   they shall have the earth for their posession.
How blest are those who .... and ....
    to see right prevail;
   they shall be satisfied.
How blest are those who show ....;
   mercy shall be shown to them.
How blest are those whose hearts are ....;
   they shall see God.
How blest are the ....;
   God shall call them his sons.
How blest are those who have suffered .... for
   the cause of right;
   the kingdom of Heaven is theirs.

(Matthew chapter 5, verses 3 to 10)

6 'What is the use of worrying; it never was worth while.' Comment on this, using Jesus's teaching in the Sermon on the Mount.

7 Jesus said he did not come to abolish but to 'fulfil' the Law of Moses and the Old Testament. Illustrate his statement from his teaching in the Sermon on the Mount about (a) murder, (b) adultery, and (c) oath-taking.

8 What did Jesus teach in the Sermon on the Mount about (a) laying up treasures on earth, (b) judging others, and (c) retaliation? Comment on *two* of these sayings, showing their importance for our lives today.

9 What did the Sermon on the Mount teach about giving alms, prayer and fasting? Is any of this teaching still of value today?

10 'When Jesus had finished his discourse the people were astounded at his teaching; unlike their own teachers he taught with a note of authority.' From the Sermon on the Mount show clearly how Jesus taught with authority.

11 Write out the version of the Lord's Prayer in Matthew's Gospel.

12 What would it mean if God's will were done on earth?
13 What did Jesus teach about marriage and divorce? Do you think his teaching is still relevant today?
14 'You have learned ... "An eye for an eye and a tooth for a tooth".' What did Jesus teach was a better way? Give a modern example of 'An eye for an eye and a tooth for a tooth'.
15 The following passage was written by the Russian, Leo Tolstoy. Read it carefully.

'"Well, but you, Leo Nikolayevich; you preach — but how about practice?" People always put it to me and always triumphantly shut my mouth with it. You preach, but how do you live? And I reply that I do not preach and cannot preach, though I passionately desire to do so. I could only preach by deeds; and my deeds are bad. What I say is not a sermon, but only a refutation of a false understanding of the Christian teaching and an explanation of its real meaning. Its meaning is not that we should in its name rearrange society by violence: its purpose is to find the meaning of our life in this world. The performance of Christ's five commandments gives that meaning. If you wish to be a Christian, you must fulfil those commands. If you do not wish to fulfil them, don't talk of Christianity.... I do not fulfil a ten-thousandth part it is true, and I am to blame for that; but it is not because I do not wish to fulfil them that I fail, but because I do not know how to. Teach me how to escape from the nets of temptation that have ensnared me, help me, and I will fulfil them; but even without help I desire and hope to do so. Blame me — I do that myself — but blame *me*, and not the path I tread, and show to those who ask me where in my opinion the road lies! If I know the road home and go along it drunk, staggering from side to side — does that make the road along which I go a wrong one? ...'

Say in what ways you agree with Tolstoy and in what ways you disagree, quoting the Sermon on the Mount to illustrate and support your views.

15   Jesus in the Synagogue at Nazareth

Jesus in the synagogue: story and comments

Every Sabbath day Jesus used to go to worship in the synagogue. He was in the synagogue at Nazareth when they brought him the Scroll to read. He read:

'The spirit of the Lord is upon me,
because he has anointed me to preach good news to the poor.
He has sent me to proclaim release to the captives and recovering of sight to the blind,
to set at liberty those who are oppressed, to proclaim the acceptable year of the Lord.'

Jesus closed the book. Then he said, 'Today this writing has been fulfilled in your hearing.'

NB: Luke says all were pleased with Jesus. But shortly afterwards he tells us that people wanted to throw him off a cliff; but Jesus passed through the midst of them unharmed. This fits in with the parallel accounts in Matthew and Mark, where he preaches in Nazareth, but people ask, 'Who is this? Do we not know his family?' Jesus observes that only in his own country does a prophet find no honour. He marvels because of their unbelief, which prevents him performing many miracles.

(Matthew chapter 13, verses 53 to 58;
Mark chapter 6, verses 1 to 6;
Luke chapter 4, verses 16 to 30)

1 The passage from Isaiah

Divine mission   The passage Jesus reads in the synagogue is quoted only in

Luke's Gospel and is from the prophet Isaiah. Jesus claims that this applies to him:

> by God's appointment he preaches to the poor and outcast;
> he restores sight to the blind;
> he frees those who are oppressed.

This is an outline of Jesus's divine mission.

2 No honour in his own country

This passage had great importance for those Christians who wondered how Jesus's own people — the Jews — could for the most part have rejected him.

Here — in a word of Jesus himself — they learn that this was only to be expected. As Jesus observed, prophets have always been honoured — except in their own country.

1 Give an account of the occasion when Jesus preached in the synagogue at Narareth. What three things do we learn from this about Jesus's own work?
2 Jesus's followers wondered why many of the Jews rejected him. How could these followers have been helped to understand this by remembering what happened to him in the Temple.
3 Jesus said, 'A prophet will always be held in honour except in his home town, and among his kinsmen and family.' Has this statement any relevance today, in your view?
4 What do you know about the synagogue?

16   The Four Kinds of Miracle

An account of a miracle of healing: story and comments

In Capernaum Jesus was preaching to many people in a room that was packed. Four men brought with them another who was paralysed. Because of the crowd they could not reach Jesus, so they removed part of the roof and let the paralysed man down to him.

Jesus saw that the four carriers believed in his power to heal the man. He turned to the paralysed man and said, 'My son, your sins are forgiven.' Some of the crowd were then angry, asking, 'How can Jesus forgive sins? Only God can forgive sins.' Jesus replied, 'It is as easy to say "I forgive your sins" as "Take up your bed and walk". To show you that the son of man has authority on earth to forgive sins' — now he turned to the paralysed man — 'I say to you, Rise, take up your bed and walk.' He immediately did so. All were amazed and glorified God.

(Mark chapter 2, verses 1 to 12;
Matthew chapter 9, verses 1 to 8;
Luke chapter 5, verses 17 to 26)

1 Three elements

Three elements are often present when Jesus performs a miracle.
These are:

Faith or trust   1 Faith or trust in Jesus. Here in the case of the paralytic man it is shown by his four carriers.

Revelation   2 Some revelation about Jesus. Here it is his claim to be the son of man, with divine power to forgive sins on earth. (This is a very unusual revelation. Jesus hardly ever openly made such claims for himself. Usually he urged others to repent so that God would forgive them. And the claim to be *son of man* — a title for God's chosen one — is very rare.)

Response   3 A response from those who are watching. Here they glorify God for what he has done through Jesus.

2 Four kinds of miracle performed by Jesus

He heals the sick.
He casts out evil spirits (demons).
He raises dead people to life.
He rules over nature.

About *half* of his miracles are healing miracles, and these have a special meaning for those who truly understand them.

3 The special meaning of the healing miracles

This depends on understanding important verses in the prophet Isaiah, chapter 29. Isaiah said:

'In that day the deaf shall hear the words of the book, and out of the gloom and darkness the eyes of the blind shall see. The meek shall obtain fresh joy in the Lord, and the poor shall exult in the Holy One of Israel.'

Isaiah's prophecy was seen as referring to the day when God's Messiah should come. Jesus repeated it when the followers of John the Baptist came to ask who he was:

'Go and tell John what you hear and see: the blind receive their sight and the lame walk, lepers are cleansed and the deaf hear, the dead are raised up and the poor have the good news preached to them.'

(Matthew chapter 11, verses 4 and 5;
Luke chapter 7, verses 22 and 23)

(Note that Jesus has added some miracles to the ones Isaiah mentions.)

The conclusion is: **healing miracles show that the Messiah has come.**

4 The other healing miracles

1 Jesus heals a leper
> (Matthew chapter 8, verses 2 and 3;
> Mark chapter 1, verses 40 to 42;
> Luke chapter 5, verses 12 and 13)

Jesus heals Peter's mother-in-law
> (Matthew chapter 8, verses 14 and 15;
> Mark chapter 1, verses 30 and 31;
> Luke chapter 4, verses 38 and 39)

Jesus heals a centurion's servant
> (Matthew chapter 8, verses 5 to 13;
> Luke chapter 7, verses 1 to 10)

Jesus heals the paralysed man (as above, page 120)

Jesus heals a woman's haemorrhage
> (Matthew 9, verses 20 to 22;
> Mark chapter 5, verses 25 to 29;
> Luke chapter 8, verses 43 to 48)

Jesus heals two blind men
> (Matthew chapter 9, verses 27 to 31)

Jesus heals a man's withered hand
> (Matthew chapter 12, verses 10 to 13;
> Mark chapter 3, verses 1 to 5;
> Luke chapter 6, verses 6 to 10)

Jesus heals the daughter of a woman of Canaan
> (Matthew chapter 15, verses 21 to 28;
> Mark chapter 7, verses 24 to 30)

Jesus heals Bartimaeus and another man who is also blind
> (Matthew chapter 20, verses 29 to 34;
> Mark chapter 10, verses 46 to 52;
> Luke chapter 18, verses 35 to 43)

These miracles all occur in Matthew's Gospel, as well as in the other two Synoptics — though not always in both.

In Mark alone   2 Two healing miracles appear in Mark alone:
A blind man at Bethsaida is healed
> (Mark chapter 8, verses 22 to 26)

A deaf and dumb man is healed
> (Mark chapter 7, verses 31 to 37)

In Luke alone   3 Four healing miracles occur in Luke alone:
Jesus heals a woman with 'a spirit of infirmity' — she could not straighten up
> (Luke chapter 13, verses 11 to 13)

Jesus heals ten lepers — one a Samaritan
(Luke chapter 17, verses 11 to 13)
Jesus heals a man with dropsy
(Luke chapter 14, verses 1 to 4)
Jesus puts back Malchus's ear, which Peter had cut off
(Luke chapter 22, verses 50 and 51)

In John alone   4 Three healing miracles occur in John alone:
Jesus heals an official's son at Capernaum
(John chapter 4, verses 46 to 54)
Jesus heals a sick man at the pool of Bethesda
(John chapter 5, verses 1 to 9)
Jesus heals a man born blind
(John chapter 9)

5 A Gospel-writer shows his special interests

Each Gospel-writer has his own special interests, as we have
seen. This emerges in the way they treat Jesus's miracles.

Luke, for example, is specially interested in Jesus and the
non-Jews — among whom he usually includes the
Samaritans. So when Jesus heals ten lepers — as recorded
by Luke in chapter 17 — only one returns to thank Jesus.
Luke reports:

> 'Now he was a Samaritan. Then said Jesus: "Were not ten
> cleansed? Where are the nine? Was no one found to
> return and give praise to God except this foreigner?" And
> he said to him, "Rise and go your way. Your faith has
> made you well."'

A Gospel for   Luke still includes the important elements in a miracle
outcasts   mentioned above — here the Samaritan is found to have
faith. But his own interests in the Gospel for outcasts appears;
and so this miracle story, told only by this Gospel, can be
compared with a parable special to this Gospel: the good
Samaritan (Luke chapter 10, verses 30 to 35).

An account of casting out demons: story and comments

A man came up to Jesus, knelt down before him and said,
'Lord, have mercy on my son, for he is an epileptic and
suffers terribly, because often he falls into the fire and often
into the water. And I brought him to your disciples, and they

could not heal him.' Jesus replied, 'O faithless and perverse
generation, how long must I be with you? How long have I to
put up with you? Bring the boy here to me.'

Then Jesus rebuked the demon inside him, the demon
came out of him and the boy was instantly cured.

The disciples then came privately to Jesus and asked,
'Why could we not cast it out?' Jesus replied, 'Because of your
small faith. For truly I say to you, if you have faith as small as a
grain of mustard seed, you will say to this mountain, "Move
from here to there", and it will move; and nothing will be
impossible to you.'

(Matthew chapter 17, verses 14 to 20;
Mark chapter 9, verses 17 to 29;
Luke chapter 9, verses 38 to 43)

1 Faith

This is one of the elements to be looked for in the miracles
performed by Jesus. Here — leaving aside the faith of the
boy's father, which parallels, for example, the faith of those
who brought the paralysed man to Jesus — the whole
miracle is used by Mark and Matthew as a peg for Jesus's
teaching about faith to his disciples.

(An interesting exercise is to compare Matthew's
statements on this matter — as given above — with the
account as found in Mark. Mark reads:

'When he had entered the house, the disciples asked him
privately, Why could we not cast it out? He replied, This
kind cannot be driven out by anything but prayer.'

Very many scholars think these words really are about the
problems many had in the early church. They tried to cast
out demons and often failed. The blame is put on the
exorcists themselves: some demons are hard to drive out —
so you must pray even more.)

2 A revelation

A revelation about Jesus is found in all the stories of casting
out demons. This is told to us in detail in a story found in
Matthew and Luke. Many Jews (and in fact non-Jews too) at
this time seem to have been able to cast out demons as Jesus
did. Some of Jesus's enemies suggested that he had entered
into an evil pact with the prince of demons. It was this prince

of demons — known as Beelzebul — who, they said, was really throwing out demons on Jesus's behalf.

Jesus denied this. First he asked:

'If I cast out demons by Beelzebul, by whom do your sons cast them out?'

Then he told them what these miracles really meant:

'If it is by the spirit of God that I cast out demons, then the kingdom of God has come upon you.'

(Matthew chapter 12, verses 24 to 29;
Luke chapter 11, verses 15 to 20)

So, casting out demons is a sign that the kingdom of God has arrived.

3 A response

In the account on pages 123–4, Luke is the Gospel-writer who includes a response by those standing by. He omits all discussion of why the disciples could not cast out this particular demon. He replaces this by the statement, 'And all were astonished at the majesty of God.' Here is the

Power of God   recognition of God's power acting through Jesus.

4 Demons and modern medicine

The story given on pages 123–4 is interesting because it assumes the sick boy is an epileptic, subject to epileptic fits. Many people today suffer from epilepsy and epileptic fits, but we no longer suppose that these are caused by demons inside them. So these stories of casting out demons raise problems for modern readers of the Bible.

You can see the same problem in some other stories of this kind.

Mark, in chapter 9, verses 17 to 29, tells us:

A deaf and dumb boy with an evil spirit

'One of the crowd said to Jesus: "Teacher, I have brought my son to you, for he has a dumb spirit; and wherever it seizes him, it dashes him down; and he foams and grinds his teeth and becomes rigid; and I asked your disciples to cast it out, but they could not."'

Jesus condemns the disciples for their faithlessness. He says to the boy's father that anything is possible to people who believe. The man cries, 'Lord, I believe; help my unbelief.' Then Jesus rebukes the demon, saying, 'You dumb and deaf spirit, I command you, come out of him and never enter him again.' And the boy is healed. Then Jesus explains to the disciples why they failed to heal the deaf, dumb child.

Again, no one today would claim that a deaf and dumb person was possessed by an evil spirit. Jesus — as a man of his time — clearly did. Here he even talks to the unclean spirit.

Do we need to believe exactly what Jesus did in order to learn from this miracle (and others like it) what he taught **Faith**   about faith?

5 The spirits recognise Jesus

In the eyes of the Gospel-writers, these evil spirits, coming from the unseen world, recognise things about Jesus unseen by others. Here is one such occasion when Jesus was teaching in the synagogue

A man with an   A man with an unclean spirit cried out, 'What have you to do
unclean spirit   with us, Jesus of Nazareth? Have you come to destroy us? I know who you are, you holy one of God.' Jesus rebuked the unclean spirit and said, 'Shut up. Come out of him.' The man was convulsed by the unclean spirit as it came out, and he cried with a loud voice. Everyone was amazed. They said, 'He commands even the unclean spirits with authority, and they obey him.'

(Mark chapter 1, verses 23 to 26;
Luke chapter 4, verses 33 to 36)

Now in both Gospels Jesus has just been teaching and people are amazed at his authority.

The unclean   The unclean spirit recognises where that authority comes
spirit   from. Jesus teaches with authority because he is the
recognises   Messiah. The spirit here speaks for *all* spirits of evil. ('Have
Jesus's   you come to destroy *us*?', it asks, not just 'me'.) The spirit,
authority   though evil, is seen by the Gospel-writers as having supernatural sight, able to penetrate behind the ordinary events to see what is really happening with the coming of Jesus.

6 The other miracles where Jesus casts out demons

Jesus casts the evil spirit into pigs

(Matthew chapter 8, verses 28 to 34;

Mark chapter 5, verses 1 to 15;

Luke chapter 8, verses 27 to 35)

Jesus heals a man made blind and dumb by a demon

(Matthew chapter 12, verses 22 and 23)

An account of the raising of the dead: story and comments

A ruler of the synagogue came to Jesus and said, 'My daughter has just died. Even so, come and lay your hand on her and she will live.'

When Jesus reached the man's house, he saw people making a great noise in mourning. He said: 'Go away; the girl is not dead. She is asleep.' They laughed. But when they had been sent out, Jesus took the girl's hand, and said, 'Little girl, arise.' She immediately got up and walked; and everyone was overcome with amazement.

(Matthew chapter 9, verses 18, 19, 23 to 25;

Mark chapter 5, verses 22 to 24, 38 to 42;

Luke chapter 8, verses 41, 42, 49 to 56)

1 Jesus brings dead people back to life only three times

The miracle of Jairus's daughter (above), the raising of the widow's son at Nain, the raising of Lazarus — all these three look forward to the greatest miracle of the New Testament, when God raised Jesus from the dead.

God is the one who usually — if not always — has power over life and death. No one supposes that Jesus *raised himself* from death. But Jesus in these three miracles displays the same power. Anyone who relies on Jesus may regard death as no more than a sleep from which he will wake them. And in so doing, he is the supreme agent of God.

2 The three elements

Faith, a revelation about Jesus, a response from those watching — all three elements are found in this miracle of the raising of Jairus's daughter.

Faith   1 The faith belongs to Jairus.

Revelation   2 The revelation is, first, that Jesus is the supreme agent of God; secondly, that one of the signs of the kingdom of God (raising the dead, as Jesus told the disciples of John the Baptist) has come to pass.

Response   3 There is a normal response of amazement.

3 The widow's son

Of the two other stories of raising the dead, one is found only in Luke's Gospel (chapter 7, verses 11 to 17) — the raising of the widow's son at Nain:

His disciples and a great crowd followed him to the city called Nain. A man who had died was being carried out of the city as Jesus came near the main gate. The body was followed by his widowed mother and a large crowd. Jesus, seeing her, had pity on her and said, 'Do not weep.'

He touched the bier on which the body lay, and said, 'Young man, I tell you, arise.' The dead man sat up and began to speak. Everyone was filled with fear. They said: 'A great prophet has arisen among us', and 'God has visited his people.'

Note that there is no stress here on faith. But we find:

1 a revelation — expressed in two sayings — of who Jesus is;
2 a response — of fear — from the crowd.

And of course once again this raising of the dead is a sign of the coming of the kingdom of God.

4 The third story of raising a person from the dead

This occurs only in John's Gospel (John chapter 11, verses 1 to 44).

Resurrection theme

This story contains striking parallels with the resurrection of Jesus (Lazarus, like Jesus, even spends the same amount of time, three days, in the tomb).

I am

The story also fits in with the special pattern of John's Gospel, enabling Jesus to utter one of his most famous 'I am' sayings: 'I am the resurrection and the life.'

It also contains the three elements of these stories:

The Resurrection of Lazarus, Uffizi Gallery, Italy

1 Faith
   'Do you believe?', Jesus asks Martha the sister of
   Lazarus. She replies, 'Yes, Lord; I believe you are the
   Christ, the son of God, he who is coming into the world.'
2 A revelation about Jesus
   The Gospel-writer himself says that the illness and death
   of Lazarus was designed 'for the glory of God and so that
   the son of God may be glorified by means of it'.
3 A response
   'Many of the Jews who had come with Mary and had
   seen what Jesus did, believed in him; but some of them
   went to the Pharisees and told them what Jesus had
   done.' (verses 45 and 46). The reaction to Jesus was
   violently divided.

An account of Jesus ruling over nature: story and comments

While Jesus prayed, the disciples went away in a boat.
When they were a long way out to sea, he came to them,
walking on the water. They were terrified. They said, 'It is a
ghost.' Jesus replied, 'Take heart. It is I. Do not be afraid.'
   Peter said, 'If it is you, Lord, command me to come to you
on the water.' Jesus said, 'Come.' Peter got out of the boat
and walked towards Jesus on the water. Then he saw the
wind, was afraid, and began to sink. He cried, 'Lord, save
me!' Jesus immediately stretched out his hand and caught
Peter, saying, 'O man of little faith! Why did you doubt?'
   They got into the boat and the wind ceased. The disciples
worshipped Jesus, saying, 'Truly you are the son of God.'
                    (Matthew chapter 14, verses 22 to 33;
                         Mark chapter 6, verses 45 to 52;
                         John chapter 6, verses 16 to 21)

**The three
elements**

Here again are the three elements:

   a word about faith (in this case Peter's lack of it);
   a revelation about Jesus ('the son of God');
   a response (Jesus is worshipped).

1 Revelation

Here is also a deeper revelation found (as we shall see, page 132), in other nature miracles.

The Old Testament asserts:

that God has power to make his way through the sea and his 'path through the great waters' (Psalm 77, verse 19);
that God alone 'trampled the waves of the sea' (Job chapter 9, verse 8);
that the Lord 'makes a way in the sea and a path in the mighty waters' (Isaiah chapter 43, verse 16).

Jesus now demonstrates that he too has these powers. Who, then, is he?

2 Another nature miracle

The same relationship with the Old Testament is seen very clearly in another nature miracle:

Jesus and his disciples were in a boat. He was asleep on a cushion in the stern when great waves arose, filling the boat.

The disciples woke Jesus, crying, 'Teacher, do you not care if we perish?' He rebuked the wind, and said to the waves, 'Peace, be still!' The wind died down; there was a great calm.

To his disciples Jesus said, 'Why are you afraid? Have you no faith?' They were filled with awe and asked each other, 'Who is this that even the wind and the sea obey him?'

(Matthew chapter 8, verses 23 to 27;
Mark chapter 4, verses 35 to 41;
Luke chapter 8, verses 22 to 25)

Note here:

faith;
a revelation;
a response.

And note the Old Testament references to God, especially from the Psalms:

'Thou dost rule the raging of the sea;
when its waves rise, thou stillest them.'

(Psalm 89, verse 9)

'He made the storm be still,
and the waves of the sea were hushed.'

(Psalm 107, verse 29)

The answer to the disciples' question 'Who is this?' is obvious to readers of the Gospels who also know the Jewish scriptures.

3 The other nature miracles in the Gospels

A coin is found in a fish's mouth

(Matthew chapter 17, verses 24 to 27)

The fig tree withers

(Matthew chapter 21, verses 18 to 22;
Mark chapter 11, verses 12 to 14, 20 and 21)

Jesus arranges a great catch of fish

(Luke chapter 5, verses 1 to 11;
John chapter 21, verses 1 to 11)

Jesus turns water into wine

(John chapter 2, verses 1 to 11)

Jesus feeds four thousand people

(Matthew chapter 15, verses 32 to 38;
Mark chapter 8, verses 1 to 9)
Jesus feeds five thousand people
(Matthew chapter 14, verses 15 to 21;
Mark chapter 6, verses 35 to 44;
Luke chapter 9, verses 12 to 17;
John chapter 6, verses 5 to 13)

4 Feeding the five thousand

Many followed Jesus across the sea of Galilee and into the hills, where he sat down with his disciples. It was the time of the Jewish feast of the Passover. Jesus, seeing so many people, asked his disciple Philip how they could possibly buy enough bread to feed so many people. (He was merely testing Philip; he himself knew what he was going to do.) Philip said 200 denarii would not be enough to buy everyone even a little. Then his disciple Andrew brought a boy who had five loaves and two fishes. On Jesus's orders, the disciples told everyone to sit down. Jesus took the loaves and gave thanks to God for them. He gave them out to those who were sitting down. He did the same with the fish. When everyone had eaten enough, Jesus ordered his disciples to collect everything that was left. They did so, and what was left filled twelve baskets.

In all four Gospels

Eucharist and Last Supper

Note that this miracle is the *only* one told in all four Gospels. The reason is that it fitted in with what happened in every Christian community — the Eucharist; that is, the repetition of Jesus's Last Supper with his disciples before his crucifixion. Points to support this:

1 Jesus's Last Supper took place at the time of the Jewish feast of the Passover. So did the feeding of the five thousand.
2 Jesus's actions — taking, blessing and distributing the bread and fishes — correspond exactly with what he did at the Last Supper.
3 There are twelve baskets left: the twelve Apostles, and no doubt their followers too, are to carry on distributing this miraculous bread. (NB: The fishes have dropped out here: no fishes were essential to the Christian Eucharist.)

Related to life of the church

All four Gospel-writers wanted to show that Jesus's life on earth was continued in the life of the church now. This clearly influenced what they put into their Gospels. Feeding the five thousand so clearly related to the weekly worship of Christians that it was seen by all four Gospel-writers as an essential element in their books.

The Messiah was expected to preside over a great feast for all his followers. This miracle shows that happening already in Jesus's life on earth. The feeding of the five thousand is a Messianic Banquet. All those who for centuries had longed for the Messiah hoped one day to sit down and eat at this banquet. Now those who came to Jesus had found the Messiah and were already sharing his feast.

1 Divide the miracles of Jesus into four kinds. Give an example of each kind.
2 When Jesus performed a miracle, he expected a response from those present. Describe *two* miracles and the people's response.

3 Write down a miracle story in which faith played an important part. How far do you think faith can work miracles today?

4 'If it is by the Spirit of God that I drive out the devils, then be sure that the kingdom of God has already come upon you.' On what occasion did Jesus make this remark, and in response to what accusation?

5 The Gospels claim that Jesus could cast out demons. What do you think modern medicine would say about these stories?

6 Describe how Jesus (a) stilled a storm; (b) raised Jairus's daughter. What difficulties do these two miracles present, and how would you try to deal with these difficulties?

7 'The blind receive their sight, the lame walk, lepers are cleansed . . . the dead are raised up.' Describe briefly three miracles recorded by Luke to show how Jesus fulfilled three of these prophecies.

8 What happened when Jesus had to deal with (a) an epileptic boy, and (b) a crowd of five thousand? Mention one problem which narratives such as these may cause, and state briefly how you would deal with it.

9 Give an account of what happened when Jesus healed (a) a young girl or boy, and (b) someone suffering from blindness or leprosy. Show how faith plays its part in the stories.

17   The Parables of Jesus

The marriage feast: story and comments

The kingdom of heaven, Jesus said, is like a king who gave a marriage feast for his son. He sent his servants to fetch those who had been invited. They would not come. They made light of the invitation, even though the king sent his servants again, with the message that everything was ready — the food all prepared. Some even killed his servants. The king was angry. He sent troops to kill the murderers and burn down their city. Then he made his servants go out into the streets and invite as many as they could find. The servants brought back anyone they could find, bad people and good people, so that the wedding was filled with guests. 'I tell you,' said the king, 'none of those who were invited shall taste my banquet.'

(Matthew chapter 22, verses 2 to 10;
Luke chapter 14, verses 16 to 24)

1 The banquet

As we already know, the heavenly banquet stands for the good time that will be brought by the coming of the kingdom of God. Jesus put much of his teaching into the form of arresting stories, always with a very sharp point. Here he is taking the traditional symbol of the kingdom of God and altering it in his own way. (Matthew's version begins as above; Luke's version begins, 'Blessed is he who shall eat bread in the kingdom of God.')

2 The point

A parable almost always has one point. Here Jesus is

contrasting those who were first offered the good news of
God's kingdom — the ancient Jews — with those who finally
arrive at the banquet. There is a parallel here with his
attitude to the so-called 'righteous' persons (Pharisees,
Sadducees, scribes, etc.) and the 'sinners' (tax collectors,
outcasts, etc.) that we have seen elsewhere. Luke's version is
more pointed than Matthew's — the last sentence in the
story above comes from Luke — perhaps because Luke is
especially concerned with the Gospel for outcasts, even for
Gentiles.

Parables of the kingdom

**Matthew
chapter 13**

By no means all Jesus's parables start by stating that they are
about the kingdom of God (or 'kingdom of heaven', as
Matthew calls it). But the parables of the kingdom of God
form the largest group of all. Matthew chapter 13, for
instance, groups together seven such parables:

the parable of the sower;
the parable of the grain of mustard seed;
the parable of the leaven in three measures of flour;
the parable of the treasure in the field;
the parable of the pearl of great value;
the parable of the dragnet;
the parable of the wheat and the weeds.

Parables as containing secrets

There is an element of a spy-story in Jesus's use of parables.
Spies speak to each other in codes. Anyone who knows the
secret formula knows the truth; but those who are ignorant of
the formula remain ignorant of the truth.

Matthew chapter 13, verses 10 and 11, records some
words of Jesus about the parables of the kingdom (also found
in Mark chapter 4 and Luke chapter 8):

Then the disciples came and said to him, 'Why do you
speak to them in parables?' And he answered them, 'To
you it has been given to know the secrets of the kingdom
of heaven, but to them it has not been given.'

Parables have a meaning that is obvious to people who can look behind the surface meaning of the story — but those who only listen to the story never see the spiritual meaning.

Ten messages in the parables

Once we know that Jesus almost always told his parables to illustrate some secret about the kingdom of God, we can then divide them up into different kinds.

A brilliant German scholar, named Joachim Jeremias, listed ten messages in the parables of Jesus:

1 Now is the Day of Salvation
2 God's mercy for sinners
3 The great assurance
4 In sight of disaster
5 It may be too late
6 The challenge of the hour
7 Being a disciple now
8 The way of sorrows and the son of man raised up
9 The end of it all
10 Actions as parables

1 Now is the Day of Salvation

Jesus said, 'Learn a lesson from the fig tree. As soon as its branch becomes tender and puts out leaves, you know that summer is near. So it is that when you see what I have described taking place — the sun will go dark; the moon will give no light; the powers of heavens will shake — you know that he is near, at the very gates.'

(Matthew chapter 24, verses 29 to 33;
Mark chapter 13, verses 24 to 29;
Luke chapter 21, verses 25 to 31)

The parable insists that those looking for the coming of the Messiah must keep awake: be alert.

Just as the parable of the marriage feast uses Old Testament imagery (there, the idea of the great feast), so now Jesus takes pictures from the Old Testament:

'For the starts of the heavens and their constellations will
not give their light;
the sun will be dark at its rising
and the moon will not shed its light.'

Isaiah
                                        Isaiah chapter 13, verse 10

Clearly this parable must have been first addressed to Jews
who knew this Old Testament saying by heart.

2 God's mercy for sinners

Jesus told this parable: 'What man of you, who has one
hundred sheep and loses one of them, will not leave the
ninety-nine alone in the desert and look for the lost one till
he finds it? When he has found it he lays it on his shoulders
with joy. When he comes home he calls together his friends
and neighbours, saying, "Rejoice with me; I have found the
sheep which was lost."'

Jesus added: 'Similarly, I tell you, there will be more
happiness in heaven over one sinner who is sorry for his sins
than over ninety-nine just people who don't need to be
sorry.'

(Matthew chapter 18, verses 12 to 14;
Luke chapter 15, verses 3 to 7)

The point of the parable is clearly stated by Jesus at the end.
The account above is taken from Luke's version of this
parable. Luke begins by saying:

'Now the tax collectors and sinners were all drawing near
to hear him. And the Pharisees and the scribes grumbled,
saying, "This man receives sinners and eats with them."'

Luke therefore sets this parable in the context of the
long-standing quarrel between Jesus and the 'righteous ones'
in the Judaism of his time.
  Other parables dealing with this theme are very important
and often very moving. They include:

the parable of the lost coin (Luke chapter 15, verses 8 to
10);
the parable of the prodigal son (Luke chapter 15, verses
11 to 32);
the parable of the Pharisee and the tax collector (Luke
chapter 18, verses 9 to 14).

3 The great assurance

Jesus said, 'A sower went out sowing. Some of his seed fell along the path. Birds came and ate it. Some fell on rocky ground. For a short time it sprang up, but it had no soil for its roots and soon died, when the sun burnt it. Some fell among thorns. The thorns choked it. Some fell into good ground: it produced thirty, sixty, even one hundred times its own weight in grain.'

(Matthew chapter 13, verses 3 to 8;
Mark chapter 4, verses 3 to 8;
Luke chapter 8, verses 5 to 8)

Later on the church would see this parable as explaining why many one-time Christians fell away from the faith. You can see this in the explanations of the parable offered in the Gospels (which, remember, were written long after Jesus told his parable).
You can read them in:

- Matthew chapter 13, verses 18 to 23;
- Mark chapter 3, verses 13 to 20;
- Luke chapter 8, verses 11 to 15.

But initially the parable had one point:

the word of God, sown in the world, will produce far more fruit than anyone could ever hope for.

Other parables dealing with this theme are:

seedtime to harvest
(Mark chapter 4, verses 26 to 29);
the grain of mustard seed
(Matthew chapter 13, verses 31 to 32;
Mark chapter 4, verses 30 to 32;
Luke chapter 13, verses 18 to 19).

4 In sight of disaster

Jesus said:

'A rich farmer had land which produced so much that he had nowhere to store all his crops. He said, "I will pull down my barns and build bigger ones. Then I shall tell my soul to eat, drink and be merry." But God said. "You fool!

Tonight your soul will be asked for. Where will your barns be then?"' Jesus ended his parable: 'So is he who lays up treasure for himself and is not rich in the sight of God.'

(Luke chapter 12, verses 16 to 21)

The kingdom of God brings joy to those who shall enter it. To those kept out it brings judgments.

This parable speaks of that judgment and warns people to watch out for it.

Other parables in the Gospels are addressed especially to certain groups of people, warning them that they are close to disaster. Amongst these parables are:

the parable of the doorkeeper (Mark chapter 13, verses 33 to 37; Luke chapter 12, verses 35 to 38) addressed especially to the scribes;
the parable of the blind leading the blind (Matthew chapter 15, verse 14; Luke chapter 6, verse 39) addressed especially to the Pharisees.

5 It may be too late

Jesus said:

'The kingdom of heaven is like ten maidens, all waiting for a bridegroom to arrive at his wedding. They have lamps lit with oil. Five took no spare oil with them. The other five took extra oil. They were all asleep, because the bridegroom was late. Suddenly there was a cry: "Here is the bridegroom! Come and meet him!" Those without oil tried in vain to borrow oil from those who had kept some extra. They had to go and buy more. While they were away the bridegroom arrived. When they got back, the door to the wedding feast had been shut. The man in charge would not let them in.'

Jesus added:

'Watch, therefore, for you know neither the day nor the hour.'

(Matthew chapter 25, verses 1 to 13)

The word 'Watch' is what counts here. This parable is found only in Matthew, but here is one found in Luke as well:

'A thief comes to steal from a house. If the householder had

known in what part of the night the thief was coming, he
would have watched and not let his house be broken into.'
(Matthew chapter 24, verse 43;
Luke chapter 12, verse 39)

The fig tree   Another parable with this theme is the parable of the fig tree
(Luke chapter 13, verses 6 to 9). The interesting point about
this parable is that a little more time is granted. But
essentially it has the same meaning and point.

6 The challenge of the hour

Jesus said:

'There was a rich man, clothed in purple clothing who ate
wonderfully every day. Outside his house lay a poor man
named Lazarus. He was covered in sores. He longed to eat
the bits that fell from the rich man's table. But all that
happened was dogs came to lick his sores.
'The poor man died. He went to heaven. The rich man
died. He went to hell. He saw into heaven and begged that
Lazarus might bring him a tiny drop of water, but the
answer was No. The rich man had good things once;
Lazarus had nothing. Now everything was reversed.
Between them was a great gulf. Lazarus was not even
allowed to go to warn the rich man's brothers about their
future fate. (After all, the message was there in the Law
and the Prophets.)'
(Luke chapter 16, verses 19 to 31)

This is a 'two-edged' parable: the contrast between the fates
of the two men in this world and then in the next is very
pointed. William Barclay called this parable 'The Punishment
of the Man who Never Noticed.' He commented:

'The sin of the rich man was that he could look on the
world's suffering and need and feel no answering sword of
grief and pity in his heart; he looked at a fellow-man,
hungry and in pain, and did nothing about it. His was the
punishment of the man who never noticed.'
(*The Daily Bible Study: The Gospel of Saint Luke* Saint
Andrew Press, Edinburgh)

In short, the rich man, failing to accept the challenge of the
hour, is himself rejected by God.
Here is another parable about the same theme:

'Strive to enter by the narrow door, for many, I tell you, will seek to enter and will not be able. When once the householder has shut the door, you will stand outside and knock in vain, crying, "Lord, please let us in." He will answer, "I do not know where you come from . . ."'

(Luke chapter 13, verses 24 to 29)

7 Being a disciple now

Jesus said:

'The kingdom of heaven is like a treasure hidden in a field. A man finds it and then quickly buries it again. Then, with great joy, he goes and sells everything he owns in order to buy that field.'

(Matthew chapter 13, verse 44)

This parable is about not wasting time, money, emotion or desire on anything except seizing the chance to be one of God's chosen disciples. We see here (wrote C H Dodd in his book *The Parbles of the Kingdom*) 'a man suddenly confronted with a treasure of inestimable worth, which he forthwith acquires at the cost of all he has.' A second parable, setting out precisely the same point, follows immediately in Matthew's Gospel:

'Again,' said Jesus, 'the kingdom of heaven is like a merchant in search of fine pearls, who, when he had discovered one pearl of enormous value, went and sold all that he had and bought it.'

(Matthew chapter 13, verses 45 and 46)

8 The way of sorrows and the son of man raised up

Jesus said:

'I am the good shepherd. The good shepherd lays down his life for the sheep. The hired hand, who is not a shepherd, who does not own the sheep, sees a wolf coming and runs away. The wolf snatches and scatters the sheep. As the good shepherd I know those sheep that belong to me — and they know me — just as my Father knows me and I know my Father. And I lay down my life for the sheep.'

(John chapter 10, verses 11 to 15)

John's Gospel always stresses that Jesus is in charge of all events — even those when he suffers. So the shepherd *deliberately* gives his life to save his sheep. This is a parable of the meaning of Jesus's crucifixion. He deliberately dies, John believes, to save mankind. This is part of the mystery of the crucifixion, and John expresses it here in a parable. The death of the shepherd is not wasted.

You can find this very difficult thought expressed in other Gospel parables, for instance:

'The stone which the builders rejected has become the main cornerstone.'

(Mark chapter 12, verse 10)

Jesus takes this image from Psalm 118, verse 22.

9 The end of it all

Jesus said:

'The kingdom of heaven is like a man who sowed good seed in his field. Then his enemy came and sowed weeds among the wheat. When everything grew, the weeds came up with the good wheat. The man's servants came and asked whether they should go to gather up the wheat. The man said No. Let both wheat and weeds grow together till harvest time. Then I will tell the reapers to burn the weeds and gather the wheat into my barn.'

(Matthew chapter 13, verses 24 to 30)

The Last Judgment

This is a parable of the Last Judgment (though there is a hint of the time granted for repentance in the parable of the ten maidens, referred to in number 5, page 140, above). However, Matthew clearly sees it as a parable about judgment. Later in the chapter, when the disciples ask Jesus what this parable means, he replies that 'at the close of the age the son of man will send his angels to gather out of his kingdom all causes of sin and all evil doers, to throw them into the furnace of fire. Men will weep there and gnash their teeth. But the righteous will shine like the sun in the kingdom of their Father.' And a parable with exactly the same point follows almost immediately:

the parable of the dragnet

(Matthew chapter 13, verses 47 to 50).

10 Actions as parables

The disciples were discussing who was the greatest among them. Jesus took a child and put him among them all. He said: 'Whoever receives one such child in my name receives me; and whoever receives me, receives not me but him who sent me.'

(Mark chapter 9, verses 34 to 37)

The disciples asked Jesus who is the greatest in the kingdom of heaven. He called a child, put the child among them all and said: 'Truly I tell you, unless you transform yourselves and become like children, you will never enter the kingdom of heaven. Whoever humbles himself like a child, he is the greatest in the kingdom of heaven.'

(Matthew chapter 18, verses 1 to 4)

An argument arose among the disciples about which of them was the greatest. Jesus took a child and made him stand next to him. He said, 'Whoever receives this child in my name receives me, and whoever receives me receives him who sent me; for he who is least among you is the one who is great.'

(Luke chapter 9, verses 46 to 48)

This 'acted parable' obviously puzzled the Gospel-writers and those from whom they learned about this story.

- For Mark the point is one's attitude towards children.
- For Matthew the point is imitating the virtues of children.
- For Luke the point seems to be a mixture of both: one's attitude towards children; and imitating the virtues of children.

Other acted parables are:

washing the disciples' feet

(John chapter 13, verses 1 to 20)

riding into Jerusalem on an ass

(Matthew chapter 21, verses 1 to 9;
Mark chapter 11, verses 1 to 10;
Luke chapter 19, verses 29 to 38)

Rules for understanding the meaning of a parable

Look for main point

1 Above all, look for the main point. Don't be led astray by working out the meaning of the entrancing details that Jesus (or the Gospel-writers, or others before them) have included.
A parable is a story with one point — addressed straight to people's hearts.
2 Ask who is being addressed. Is it the disciples? Is it the scribes or the Pharisees?
3 Ask whether the Christians who transmitted any parable to the Gospel-writer many years after Jesus told it might have altered it to fit in with their own problems and circumstances.
4 Try to work out whether the Gospel-writers, in giving the meaning of a parable, might have got it wrong. This means:
comparing the interpretation with the parable itself;
looking to see if a different Gospel gives a different interpretation of the same parable.
But above all, look for the main point.

Lists of parables and their sources

1 Parables found in the three Synoptic Gospels

The lamp under a bed
(Matthew chapter 5, verses 14 and 15;
Mark chapter 4, verses 21 and 22;
Luke chapter 8, verse 16)
The houses built on rock and sand
(Matthew chapter 7, verses 24 to 27;
Luke chapter 6, verses 47 to 49)
New cloth on old clothes
(Matthew chapter 9, verse 16;
Mark chapter 2 verse 21;
Luke chapter 5, verse 36)
The sower
(Matthew chapter 13, verses 3 to 8;
Mark chapter 4, verses 3 to 8;
Luke chapter 8, verses 5 to 8)

New wine bursts old wineskins
> (Matthew chapter 9, verse 17;
> Mark chapter 2, verse 22;
> Luke chapter 5, verses 37 and 38)

The mustard seed
> (Matthew chapter 13, verses 31 and 32;
> Mark chapter 4, verses 30 to 32;
> Luke chapter 13, verses 18 and 19)

The yeast
> (Matthew chapter 13, verse 33;
> Luke chapter 13, verses 20 and 21)

The lost sheep
> (Matthew chapter 18, verses 12 and 13;
> Luke chapter 15, verses 4 to 6)

The wicked tenants
> (Matthew chapter 21, verses 33 to 41;
> Mark chapter 12, verses 1 to 9;
> Luke chapter 20, verses 9 to 16)

The fig tree promises summer
> (Matthew chapter 24, verses 32 and 33;
> Mark chapter 13, verses 28 and 29;
> Luke chapter 21, verses 29 to 32)

The parable of the talents
> (Matthew chapter 25, verses 14 to 30;
> Luke chapter 19, verses 12 to 27)

2 Ten parables found only in Matthew

The wheat and the weeds
> (Matthew chapter 13, verses 24 to 30)

The hidden treasure
> (Matthew chapter 13, verse 44)

The pearl
> (Matthew chapter 13, verses 45 and 46)

The dragnet
> (Matthew chapter 13, verses 47 and 48)

The unjust servant
> (Matthew chapter 18, verses 23 to 35)

The workers
> (Matthew chapter 20, verses 1 to 16)

The two sons
> (Matthew chapter 21, verses 28 to 31)

The man without a wedding garment
> (Matthew chapter 22, verses 11 to 14)

The ten bridesmaids
(Matthew chapter 25, verses 1 to 13)
The sheep and the goats
(Matthew chapter 25, verses 31 to 46)

3 One parable found only in Mark

The unexpected harvest
(Mark chapter 4, verses 26 to 29)

4 Eighteen parables found only in Luke

A creditor and two debtors
(Luke chapter 7, verses 41 to 43)
The good Samaritan
(Luke chapter 10, verses 30 to 37)
The friend in need
(Luke chapter 11, verses 5 to 8)
The rich fool
(Luke chapter 12, verses 16 to 21)
The men waiting for their master
(Luke chapter 12, verses 35 to 40)
The faithful steward
(Luke chapter 12, verses 42 to 48)
The barren fig tree
(Luke chapter 13, verses 6 to 9)
The guests who wanted the best seats
(Luke chapter 14, verses 7 to 14)
The marriage banquet
(Luke chapter 14, verses 16 to 24)
A man who builds without enough money to finish his
building
(Luke chapter 14, verses 28 to 30)
Working out whether you can win a battle
(Luke chapter 14, verses 31 to 33)
The lost coin
(Luke chapter 15, verses 8 to 10)
The prodigal son
(Luke chapter 15, verses 11 to 32)
The dishonest steward
(Luke chapter 16, verses 1 to 8)
The rich man and poor Lazarus
(Luke chapter 16, verses 19 to 31)

How servants should be treated
(Luke chapter 17, verses 7 to 10)
The widow who would not give up
(Luke chapter 18, verses 2 to 5)
The Pharisee and the tax collector
(Luke chapter 18, verses 10 to 14)

Special insights of different Gospels as shown by their parables

1 Matthew

Matthew chapter 13 is especially important in revealing the Gospel-writer's own views about the kingdom of heaven, how God brings it to us, what we should do in response. The theme 'discovering God's will and then obeying it' is one summary of what Matthew regards as essential.

Discovering and obeying God's will

2 Luke

With Luke such parables as:

the good Samaritan;
the prodigal son;
the rich man and poor Lazarus;
the Pharisee and the tax collector

have a central meaning to his whole message. His care for outcasts, the poor, non-Jews, and so on (which we have already explored in this book) shine powerfully from these, and from other parables special to Luke's Gospel.

3 John

John's Gospel, as we have seen, is quite different in many ways from the three Synoptic Gospels. But pages 142–3, number 8 above reveals that John too uses parables in his own special way.

1 Tell the story of the *Lost Coin*. In which Gospel is it found?
2 Tell the story of the *Man without a Wedding Garment*. In which Gospel is it found?
3 Tell the story of the *Unexpected Harvest*. In which Gospel is it found?
4 Describe four types of ground in which the sower in Jesus's parable sowed his seed. Give a modern parallel which someone explaining this parable might use for each type.
5 In your own words tell the parable of the marriage banquet. What does the banquet stand for? What is the point of this parable?
6 Write an account of *one* of the parables of the kingdom.
7 'Why do you speak in parables?', the disciples asked. What was Jesus's answer? What did he mean?
8 Write out a parable warning us to be on the look-out for the coming of God.
9 Give three parables told only in Matthew's Gospel, recounting *one* fully in your own words.
10 Give four rules for understanding the meaning of a parable. Using *one* of the parables of Jesus, illustrate these four rules.
11 Tell the story of the prodigal son, and list *three* other parables found only in Luke's Gospel.
12 What do the parables of Jesus tell us about caring for outcasts today?
13 What did Jesus teach about a person's duty to forgive? In your answer mention (but do not write out) two parables of forgiveness.
14 Tell two parables of Jesus, showing how they can be of help to us today.
15 Write out a parable of your own.

18   Peter's Confession

Story and comments

Near Caesarea Philippi, Jesus asked his disciples, 'Who do people say I am?' They answered, 'Some people think you are John the Baptist; others think you are Elijah; others say you are Jeremiah or another of the prophets.'

Jesus than said, 'Who do *you* think I am?' Peter answered, 'You are the Messiah, the son of the living God.'

Jesus said, 'No human being revealed this to you, Peter. My heavenly father revealed it to you. Peter, your name means "a rock". I shall build my church on this rock; nothing — not even death — shall destroy it. You have the keys of the kingdom of heaven. Your decisions on earth will be accepted in heaven.'

Then he told them to keep what they had learned secret. He began to tell them how soon he would go to Jerusalem to suffer, be killed and rise again from the dead. Peter said, 'This must never happen to you.' Jesus replied, 'Now you are not on God's side but on the side of weak human beings. Get behind me. You speak the words of Satan.'

(Matthew chapter 16, verses 13 to 23;
Mark chapter 8, verses 27 to 33;
Luke chapter 9, verses 18 to 22)

This is a turning point in the three Synoptic Gospels: Jesus has done many wonders; many have learned from him; who can this man be to act and teach in these ways? There are three main elements in what we learn here:

1 Jesus is the Messiah

Jesus is not one of those who *come before* the Messiah (John the Baptist, Elijah or a prophet). He is the Messiah himself. Peter speaking for all the disciples, but inspired by God, recognises this.

2 Recognition of the Messiah

Those who confess that Jesus is the Messiah become leaders of Jesus's church. They have the 'keys of the kingdom'. (Later in Matthew's Gospel, chapter 18, verse 18, the power given to Peter is given to all the disciples.) To recognise that Jesus is the Messiah makes a disciple as firm as a rock.

3 Misunderstanding

People misunderstand what the Messiah must go through. They do not expect a Messiah to suffer. That is why Jesus is not willing to announce to everyone his true character. They will want a king, not a sufferer. This is made extremely clear by the reaction of Peter, when Jesus starts explaining what his role as Messiah involves.

19   The Transfiguration

Story and comments

Six days after Peter's confession Jesus took his three closest disciples, Peter, James and John, up a high mountain. There his face shone like the sun; his clothing became glistening white. And Moses and Elijah appeared, talking to him. A bright cloud came over them, and a voice from the cloud said, 'This is my beloved son, with whom I am well pleased.'

Hearing this the disciples fell down and hid their faces. Peter had wanted to build three tents, one for Jesus, one for Moses and one for Elijah, but now the disciples were afraid. Jesus said, 'Rise; have no fear.' They looked up and only Jesus was there.

As they came down the mountain Jesus said, 'Do not tell anyone what you have seen until the son of man is raised from the dead.'

(Matthew chapter 17, verses 1 to 9;
Mark chapter 9, verses 1 to 9;
Luke chapter 9, verses 28 to 36)

1 The approval of God

God is here showing that he supports, approves of and is entirely with Jesus. He is above all endorsing Jesus's understanding of what he must do as the Messiah. This Jesus explained to his disciples after Peter's confession. The words God uses are virtually the same as the voice from heaven at Jesus's baptism.

2 Why Moses and Elijah?

These two men from the Old Testament represent the law

and the prophets. Jesus now is seen as the final development
— the 'culmination' — of both.

3 The cloud

This is a symbol of God's presence in the Bible. Moses, for
instance (as Exodus chapter 40 tells us) built a tent where the
children of Israel should meet God, and a cloud covered the
tent which was filled with the glory of God.

4 Secrecy

As when Peter confessed that Jesus was the Messiah, now
again Jesus says that the disciples who have seen the
transfiguration must tell no one. People will not understand
that Jesus must still suffer, even though God has given this
great sign of approval. On this occasion there is a time limit
on the secrecy. Once Jesus *has* suffered and risen from the
dead, then they may tell what they have seen.

1 'Jesus turned round, and, looking at his disciples, rebuked
   Peter. "Away with you, Satan," he said; "you think as men
   think, not as God thinks".' Why did Jesus say this to Peter?
   Give an example from your own experience of someone
   making a wrong judgment in the same way as Peter did.
2 '"And you," he asked, "who do you say that I am?"' What
   answer did Peter give to Jesus's question? How did Jesus
   react to Peter's words?
3 Tell in your own words what the disciples saw and heard
   at the transfiguration of Jesus. What did Jesus say to them
   as they came down the mountain?
4 'They saw Elijah appear, and Moses with him, and there
   they were, conversing with Jesus.' When did this happen?
   What do you think the appearances of Elijah and Moses
   stand for?

20   The Last Supper

Story and comments

Each year the Jews celebrated the feast of the Passover and the feast of Unleavened Bread. This was to rejoice because long ago God had helped them to escape from the Egyptians. Families would gather together for a special meal.

Jesus wished to celebrate this feast for the last time with his disciples before he was killed. To keep the place where they would meet secret, he sent two disciples into Jerusalem. There they were to look for a man carrying a large jar of water. He would lead them to an upper room, furnished and ready, if they said the Teacher needed it for the Passover.

When the time came the twelve disciples and Jesus met in this upper room. Jesus knew that Judas Iscariot had gone over to the side of those who wanted to kill him. He said, 'One of you who is eating will betray me.' They all said, 'Is it I?' Jesus replied, 'I shall dip a piece of bread and give it to the one who will betray me.' He gave it to Judas Iscariot, who went out into the night.

Then Jesus broke bread and said, 'This is my body which is given for you; do this in remembrance of me.' He took a cup of wine and said, 'All of you drink this. It is my blood of a new agreement with mankind, poured out for you.' He blessed both the bread and the wine.

Then he said: 'I give you a new law: love one another the way I have loved you. By this everyone will know that you are my disciples.'

Peter asked where Jesus was going after this supper. Jesus said, 'You cannot follow me now; you will follow me later.' Peter disagreed. 'Why cannot I follow you now?' he asked. 'I will lay down my life for you,' he declared. Jesus said, 'Truly I tell you, before the cock crows in the morning you will three times have denied that you know me.'

(Matthew chapter 26, verses 17 to 35;
Mark chapter 14, verses 12 to 25;
Luke chapter 22, verses 7 to 34;
John chapter 13, verses 21 to 38)

1 Preparations for the Passover

Jesus was determined to celebrate this feast in Jerusalem, even though he knew his enemies there were ready to kill him. Clearly he had made arrangements with one of his Jerusalem followers to prepare a room with great secrecy — revealing it, by specially arranged signs and passwords, to the two disciples sent on ahead.

2 Judas Iscariot

Jesus is quoting Psalm 41, verse 9: 'He who ate my bread has lifted his heel against me.' The Gospel-writers show here Jesus's uncanny insight into his disciples' minds, for none of the eleven knows who it is that will betray Jesus. Judas leaves the table — leaving the light of Jesus's presence and going out into darkness.

Below: The Last Supper, Holy Blood Altarpiece by Tilman Riemenschneider at St Jakobskirche, Rothenburg-ob-der-Tauber, Germany

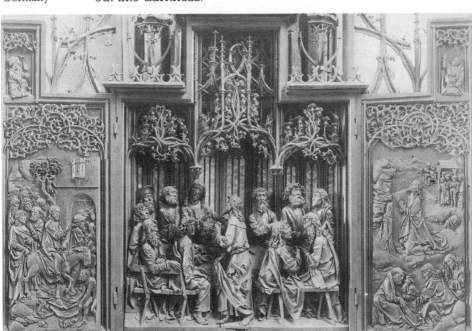

3 Breaking bread; pouring wine

From one point of view this was one of Jesus's most moving 'acted parables'. In addition it had special meaning for those later Christians reading the four Gospels, since they did obey his command and each week met for the Eucharist — repeating his words and actions with bread and wine.

4 Peter

A second betrayal, alongside that of Judas, is foretold here by Jesus. Peter thinks he can go along with Jesus even as far as death. Jesus knows Peter is not ready for this. Before morning Peter, under the strain of what will happen, will deny Jesus.

QUESTIONS

1 Fill in the missing words:

During supper Jesus took ...., and having said the blessing he broke it and gave it to the disciples with the words: 'Take this and eat; this is my ....' Then he took a ...., and having offered thanks to God he gave it to them with the words: 'Drink from it, all of you. For this is my ...., the blood of the covenant, shed for many for the forgiveness of sins. I tell you, never again shall I drink from the fruit of the vine until that day when I drink it new with you in the kingdom of my Father.'

(Matthew chapter 26, verses 26 to 29)

2 Why do Jews celebrate the feast of the Passover?
3 Where did Jesus and his disciples meet for the Last Supper? In your own words, tell what happened.
4 Christians today repeat what happened at the Last Supper in the Mass or Holy Communion. What do you think is the meaning of the bread and wine in the Mass or Holy Communion? (Quote some of Jesus's own words in your answer.)
5 What do we learn from the Gospels about (a) how Jesus and his disciples prepared for the Last Supper; (b) the Supper itself?
6 Tell what happened at the Last Supper (a) between Jesus and Judas; (b) between Jesus and Peter.

21 Jesus Betrayed and Arrested

Story and comments

Jesus and his eleven disciples sang a hymn and went out to
the Mount of Olives. They reached a place called
Gethsemane, and Jesus took Peter, James and John further
up the hill. He prayed to God that he might not have to suffer,
asking the three closest disciples to pray with him. Instead
they fell asleep. Jesus rebuked them. To his heavenly father
he said, 'Do what you will, not what I want.'

Then Judas came with a crowd of soldiers and others,
armed with clubs. They had been sent by the chief priests,
the scribes and other opponents of Jesus. Judas had told
them that he would show Jesus to them by kissing him. He
came up to Jesus and said 'Hail master!' Then he kissed him.
Jesus said, 'Friend, why are you here?'

As the soldiers were seizing Jesus, Peter drew a sword
and cut off the ear of a man called Malchus, who was a
servant of the high priest. But Jesus stopped Peter from any
more fighting, and he healed Malchus's ear.

Then they led Jesus off, and all the disciples ran away.
Peter and another disciple timidly followed Jesus, who was
brought to the courtyard of the high priest. The other
disciple knew the high priest and his servants; he persuaded
a maid at the door to let him and Peter come in. The maid
said to Peter, 'Are you not one of Jesus's servants?' He said, 'I
am not.' As he was warming himself by the fire, he was
asked again, 'Are you not one of his disciples?' He said again,
'I am not.' Then one of Malchus's relatives asked. 'Did I not
see you with Jesus at Gethsemane?' Peter again said 'No.'
Then the cock crowed. Remembering Jesus's words, Peter
went out, weeping bitterly.

(Matthew chapter 26, verses 30 to 75;
Mark chapter 14, verses 26 to 72;
Luke chapter 22, verses 39 to 62;
John chapter 18, verses 1 to 27)

Detail of *The Betrayal* by Giotto

1 Three betrayals

Although Judas Iscariot is the one who handed Jesus over to his enemies, there are three betrayals in the Gospels:

1 Peter, James and John cannot keep awake, even when Jesus is tormented with sorrow;
2 Judas betrays his master with a kiss;
3 Peter three times denies that he knows Jesus.

2 Jesus in anguish

The story of Jesus in Gethsemane (which means 'oil press')
reveals that the events about to take place are not easy for
him to contemplate. Yet he knows that he must do his
Father's will. So, when Peter decides to fight those who have
come to arrest him, Jesus stops this. He is now fully prepared
to suffer and to die.

22   Jesus on Trial

Jesus before Annas

The soldiers first lead Jesus before Annas, the father-in-law
of Caiaphas, who was high priest that year.

(John chapter 18, verses 12 to 14)

Jesus before the Council

Next Jesus is taken before the Jerusalem Council (or
Sanhedrin), presided over by the high priest Caiaphas.

He is accused of wanting to destroy the Jerusalem Temple.
To this Jesus answers nothing.

Then Caiaphas asks if Jesus claims to be the Messiah, the
son of God. Jesus replies 'I am.' (Matthew records that Jesus
replied, 'You have said so. But I tell you that later on you will
see the son of man seated at the right hand of power and
coming on the clouds of heaven.') Caiaphas tears his clothing
and says that Jesus is evilly claiming to be the son of God
and the Messiah.

Those holding Jesus now blindfold him and hit him in the
face, mockingly asking him to identify those who struck him.

In the morning the Council sentences Jesus to death and
has him taken to the Roman governor, Pontius Pilate.

(Matthew chapter 26, verses 57 to 68,
and chapter 27, verse 1;
Mark chapter 14, verses 53 to 65, and chapter 15, verse 1;
Luke chapter 22, verses 66 to 71;
John chapter 18, verse 24)

Jesus before Pontius Pilate

Pilate asks Jesus if he claims to be king of the Jews. Jesus

answers, 'You have said that.' When Pilate asks Jesus if he
has not understood that many people have accused him of
evil behaviour, he simply says nothing in reply. Pilate is
amazed. Luke tells us some of these accusations: the chief
priests and the crowds claimed Jesus was stirring up all the
people. According to John, Jesus told Pilate, 'My kingdom is
not of this world. Otherwise my servants would fight to stop
me being handed over to the Jews.'

Plate, according to Luke, said, 'I find no crime in this
man.'

(Matthew chapter 27, verses 2, and 11 to 14;
Mark chapter 15, verses 2 to 5;
Luke chapter 23, verses 1 to 5;
John chapter 18, verses 28 to 38)

Jesus before King Herod

Herod Antipas, governor of Judea on behalf of the Romans,
was then in Jerusalem. Learning that Jesus came from
Galilee, Pilate sent him for trial to Herod. This pleased
Herod, who had for a long time wanted to meet Jesus. (He
and Pilate had been enemies; now they became friends.)
Herod hoped Jesus would perform a miracle. But Jesus did
not even reply to Herod's questions. Herod therefore let his
soldiers mock Jesus. They dressed him up gorgeously. Then
Herod sent Jesus back to Pontius Pilate.

(Luke chapter 23, verses 6 to 12)

Jesus again before Pilate

Pilate tells all Jesus's accusers that he finds Jesus innocent.
He says he will punish Jesus but release him as well.

Pilate plans to please the crowd by releasing Jesus. At the
feast of the Passover it was his custom to release a criminal.
But the chief priests persuade the crowd to call instead for a
murderer named Barabbas to be released. Pilate asks them
what he should do with Jesus. They cry 'Crucify him'. Pilate
gives in (even though his wife says she has dreamed about
Jesus and thinks he is innocent). To try to escape any blame,
Pilate publicly washes his hands before the crowd, saying, 'I
am innocent of this man's blood.'

Christ Mocked by Matthias Grünewald

But he still has Jesus scourged and sends him to be crucified. The soldiers dress Jesus up in scarlet, put a crown — of thorns — on his head, put a reed (like a sceptre) into his right hand. Then they kneel before him and mock him, hitting him with the reed, and spitting at him.

Then Jesus is led away to be crucified.

(Matthew chapter 27, verses 15 to 31;
Mark chapter 15, verses 6 to 20;
Luke chapter 23, verses 13 to 25;
John chapter 18, verses 38 to 40,
and chapter 19, verses 1 to 16.)

1 Give the reasons why Jesus was (a) arrested by the high priest's messengers, and (b) sentenced to death by Pilate.

2 Tell in your own words the story of Peter denying Jesus. What does the story tell us about Peter?

3 Why did Judas betray Jesus? Could you defend Judas in any way?

4 Jesus's trials reveal (a) his great self-control; (b) his courage; (c) his confidence. Write an account of the trials, showing this.

5 Why was Pilate a weak man? Give an example of present-day weakness leading to disaster.

6 How was Jesus ill-treated at his trials? What was his response? Do you think this was the best response or could you suggest a better one?

7 Describe the trial of Jesus before Pontius Pilate. What charges were made against Jesus? How did Pilate try to avoid passing the death sentence?

8 What does Luke's account of the trial of Jesus tell us about the attitudes and characters of (a) Pontius Pilate, and (b) Herod?

9 On trial, Jesus is passed from judge to judge. Give an account of three persons (or groups of people) who judged Jesus after his arrest.

23   The Crucifixion

Story and comments

They made a cross for Jesus. He was forced to carry it
himself to where they planned to crucify him — at a spot
named Golgotha, which means 'the place of a skull'. A man
named Simon, who came from Cyrene, was forced to help
him to carry the cross.

He was offered wine to drink, but refused it. The soldiers
cast lots for his clothing.

On either side of Jesus was crucified a thief. One mocked
him, saying, 'If you are the Messiah, save yourself and us.'
The other thief rebuked this man, pointing out that they were
criminals, but Jesus had done nothing wrong. Jesus said to
this thief, when asked by him to be remembered when Jesus
came into his kingdom: 'Truly I say to you, today you will be
with me in paradise.'

Many others standing round mocked, saying, 'He saved
others, but he cannot save himself.'

Jesus's mother with her sister and with Mary Magdalene
were standing by the cross. Jesus told his disciple John that
he must now act as son to Jesus's mother. From that moment
John took Mary into his own home.

Pilate had put over Jesus's cross a notice with the words,
'The King of the Jews'. The chief priests did not like this.
They asked Pilate to write, 'This man said, I am King of the
Jews.' But Pilate replied, 'What I have written, I have written.'

Jesus hung on the cross for six hours. Of those who
crucified him he said: 'Father, forgive them; for they do not
know what they are doing.'

At one point he cried out with a very loud voice, 'My God,
my God, why have you forsaken me?' (Some people thought
he was calling on Elijah to save him at this moment.)

As Jesus died, he cried, 'It is finished,' and 'Father, into

The Deposition from the Cross by Caravaggio

your hands I commit my spirit.' And as he died the veil separating the Holy of Holies from the rest of the Jerusalem Temple was torn completely in two.

The Roman soldier in charge of those who crucified Jesus then was filled with awe. He said, 'Truly, this was the son of God.'

> (Matthew chapter 27, verses 32 to 54;
> Mark chapter 15, verses 21 to 39;
> Luke chapter 23, verses 26 to 47;
> John chapter 19, verses 17 to 30)

1 'My God, my God, why have you forsaken me?'

These are the opening words of Psalm 22. Before deciding that Jesus had finally lost his total trust in God the Father, we should read this whole Psalm. Much of it strikingly foreshadows Jesus's sufferings on the cross (so much so that some scholars have concluded that the Gospel-writers must have modified their accounts to make them fit in with this Psalm). But halfway through this Psalm the misery of the sufferer is changed into trust and hope. The Psalm says: 'But thou, O Lord, be not far off! O thou my help, hasten to my aid! Deliver my soul from the sword, my life from the power of the dog!'

In Aramaic, which Jesus spoke, the words 'My God' are 'Eli' — which explains why those watching him die thought that he was calling to Elijah for help.

2 'It is finished'

These words do not simply mean that the whole story has come to an end. They also imply that Jesus's work on earth is done — because he has achieved everything that he set out to do.

'It is finished' means 'My work is accomplished'.

3 The veil of the temple was torn in two

The Jews insisted that between God and man was a barrier that hardly any human being could penetrate. Jesus, dying on the cross, smashed that barrier. Some have suggested also that this tearing of the Temple veil from top to bottom points to the eventual destruction of the Temple itself.

1 Fill in the missing words:

Then they took him out to crucify him. A man called
............................., from Cyrene, the father of Alexander and
Rufus, was passing by on his way in from the country, and
they pressed him into service to carry his cross.
    They brought him to the place called ....
which means 'Place of a skull'. He was offered drugged
wine, but he would not take it. Then they fastened him to
the cross. They divided his .... among them,
casting lots to decide what each should have.
    The hour of the crucifixion was nine in the morning, and
the inscription giving the charge against him read, 'The
.... of the ....' Two
.... were crucified with him, one on his right
and the other on his left.

> (Mark chapter 15, verses 21 to 27)

2 On the cross of Jesus Pilate wrote a notice, saying
.... The chief priests said to Pilate, write
.... Pilate replied ....
3 'And the curtain of the Temple was torn in two from top to
bottom.' What was the meaning of this event? What other
strange happenings were recorded on this occasion?
4 On the cross Jesus cried, 'My God, my God, why hast thou
forsaken me?' Do you think that anyone can be forsaken by
God? Give reasons for your answer.
5 People today often talk about being crucified. What do
they mean? How can their sufferings be compared with
those of Jesus?
6 Describe the crucifixion of Jesus from his arrival at
Golgotha (the place of a skull) until he died. What did
Jesus say during this time?
7 Tell how on the cross Jesus (a) was despised and rejected;
(b) forgave his tormentors; (c) comforted his followers; (d)
impressed a centurion?

24   Jesus Rises from the Dead

Story and comments

1 The burial

Jesus was buried in a tomb borrowed from a Jew, Joseph of Arimathea. A great boulder was rolled before the entrance to this tomb.

In his first letter to the church at Corinth Paul gives us the first account of what happened next.

'I passed on to you, as of the greatest importance, what
  was passed on to me:
that Christ died for our sins, as the Bible foretold;
that he was buried;
that on the third day he was raised from the dead, as the
  Bible foretold;
and that he was seen by Peter and then by the twelve
  Apostles.
After that he was seen by more than five hundred
  fellow-Christians at one time — most of whom are still
  alive, though some have died.
Then he was seen by James, then by all the apostles, and
  finally he was seen by me also, as though I had been
  born at the wrong time.'

(I Corinthians chapter 15, verses 3 to 8)

2 The tomb is found empty

Later, in the Gospels, Matthew, Luke and John give stories of the resurrection. The first people to find the tomb empty were Mary the mother of James, Mary Magdalene and other women from Galilee. They had gone to the tomb to embalm

*The Three
Marys at
Christ's Tomb*
by Albrecht
Dürer

Jesus's body. The great boulder has been rolled away. There
sits an angel who says:

> 'Do not be afraid. I know you are looking for Jesus who
> was crucified. He is not here, for he has risen, as he said
> he would. Come and see the place where he lay. Then go
> quickly and tell his disciples that he has risen from the
> dead. Behold, he is going before you to Galilee. There you
> will see him.'

The women ran to tell the disciples, who did not believe
them.

(Matthew chapter 28, verses 1 to 8;
Mark chapter 16, verses 1 to 8;
Luke chapter 24, verses 1 to 11;
John chapter 20, verses 1 and 2)

3 Jesus appears to the disciples

What convinced the other disciples that Jesus had risen from death was a series of appearances he made to them. For instance:

> 'Two disciples were walking to a village called Emmaus — about seven miles outside Jerusalem. They were talking about all that had happened. Jesus drew near and started to walk with them; but they did not recognise him. They told him the whole story, including how the women had been to the tomb that morning. Jesus then explained to them how the Old Testament foretold that the Christ would suffer, and then be glorified.
>
> These two disciples persuaded this apparent stranger to eat with them. As soon as he took bread, blessed it and broke it, they recognised that he was Jesus; and he vanished.'

(Luke chapter 24, verses 13 to 31)

A kind of Eucharist

Here there is some kind of Eucharist, revealing Christ's presence. One of the appearances in John's Gospel also takes place in the setting of a meal (John chapter 21, verses 9 to 23). And another takes place on the first day of the week, when Christians usually celebrated the Eucharist (John chapter 20, verses 19 to 23). Here the Gospel-writer seems to be saying that Jesus still appears to his followers when they celebrate the meal he said would remind them of him.

1 The first person to tell us that Jesus rose from the dead was .... Who, in his account, was the first person to see the risen Jesus? Who, in his account, was the last person to see the risen Jesus?

2 The Gospels of Matthew, Luke and John tell us that the first persons to find Jesus's tomb to be empty were .... Give in your own words what they were told by an angel? What did they then do?

3 According to the Gospels, the disciples were convinced that Jesus had risen from the dead by a series of appearances by him. Describe one in your own words.

4 Retell the conversations between Jesus and (a) the thieves on the cross; and (b) Cleopas on the road to Emmaus.

5 According to the Gospel of Luke, what part was played (a) by Peter after Jesus was arrested, and (b) by the women at the tomb of Jesus?

6 Jesus often tried to change people's attitudes and beliefs. Show how he did this in (a) the parable of the rich man and Lazarus, and (b) his conversation on the road to Emmaus about the suffering of the Saviour.

7 Do you believe that Jesus rose from the dead? Do you believe that anyone can rise from the dead? Give reasons for your answers.

8 Read the accounts in the Synoptic Gospels of the events at Jesus's tomb after his burial. How do these differ?

9 'They went out and ran away from the tomb, beside themselves with terror. They said nothing to anybody, for they were afraid.' (Mark chapter 16, verse 8) Describe what the people involved had just seen and heard. How does Mark's Gospel at this point differ from the other three Gospels?

10 Show how a knowledge of the early life of Jesus may help Christians to practise their own faith today.

11 State one Christian belief which you find difficult to accept, and say why.

12 In order to be inspired by Jesus today, do you have to believe everything that is written in the Gospels about his life and teaching? Discuss.

13 Which, in your view, are the most important Christian commandments? Why do you believe this?

Coursework

1 Read the story of John the Baptist and ask yourself what it means to be a martyr. Find other people in our time who have been killed or suffered in the same way. Tell their stories.

2 Jesus said, 'Treat other people as you would like them to treat you.' Are there people who are badly treated in today's society? Describe their problems and say how you think Jesus would have treated them.

3 Jesus said, 'Unless you become as little children you will not enter the kingdom of heaven.' Give an account of the way little children behave in junior schools, in nurseries and in your own home. Are they always perfect? What did Jesus mean?

4 Jesus wanted to save people from their sins. The Parable of the Prodigal Son, for example, is about welcoming back an outcast. Give examples of people who offend us today. Describe the work of some of those people who try to save them.

5 'You are my friend', said Jesus, 'if you do what I command you.' Tell in your own words the work of those people who are trying to follow his commands today.

6 Jesus cared especially for the status of women in society. In what ways, if any, do you think women today are still seen as unimportant? Describe some women who have made major contributions to our present world.

Index

By the same authors:

Christianity

- Concise but thorough treatment with close reference to GCSE requirements
- A thought-provoking study of the themes and aspects of Christianity over the centuries and today
- Examines and explains in detail the major Catholic, Protestant, Orthodox and Anglican traditions
- Encourages pupils to asses the importance of Christianity today and to express their own views on Christian teaching, morality and practice
- Varied suggestions for coursework, guided by the GCSE national criteria, accompany each chapter
- Students are encouraged to show what they **know**, what they **understand** and how they can **evaluate** the material

ISBN 0 582 22342.3